History of Women in the Pennsylvania House of Representatives 1923-2001

The Suffrage movement, biographies,
history of statewide women's organizations
and the demographics of the 105 women
who have been elected to serve
in the state House of Representatives

Office of Speaker of the House
Matthew J. Ryan

Written by
Jeanne H. Schmedlen

The Pennsylvania House of Representatives
Harrisburg
2001

Published by the
Pennsylvania House of Representatives,
in Pennsylvania, United States of America, 2001

ISBN 0-9667794-2-8

Cover Photo

Photo from the Chatham College Archives. Students from Pennsylvania College for Women, now Chatham College, rode in a 1914 parade in Pittsburgh, in support of women's suffrage. Chatham College was founded in 1869 and is one of the oldest women's colleges in the country. Chatham student have always been active in politics – volunteering for political campaigns and working to register voters. The Center for Women in Politics in Pennsylvania at Chatham College works to involve women in the political process across the state.

Printed by Armstrong Printery, Inc., Harrisburg, PA

To the fine, dedicated women who have been elected to serve in the Pennsylvania House of Representatives. Their strength, determination and vision are an inspiration to all Pennsylvanians.

MATTHEW J. RYAN
The Speaker

History of Women in the
Pennsylvania House of Representatives
1923-2001

Table of Contents

cknowledgements

Many people and several institutions have contributed to the success of this project, which began in the fall of 1998.

First, several splendid college students serving internships in the Speaker's Office researched much of the history of the women. These interns include: Christopher D. Belen (Millersville University), Jennifer A. Clark (Elizabethtown College), Kristi Gilbert (Westminster College), Jolene Goodman (Shippensburg University), Norah E. Griffiths (Hollins University), Leigh McCuen (Temple University), Jessica Meredith (Pennsylvania State University), Rebecca L. Nicholson (Westminster College), Sarah Rajca (Edinboro University), Megan Semuta (West Chester University), and, Steve Winnie (Mansfield University and now at Cornell Law School).

Three interns deserve special mention. The first is Paul Rego (Millersville University), whose term paper about the history of the women's movement in Pennsylvania, was a great resource in the drafting of the section about suffrage. The second is Colleen Tigue (East Stroudsburg University) who carefully researched and compiled demographic statistics about the women who have served in the House. Last, little Gwen Stettler (Slippery Rock University) who also prepared an excellent document about current politics and women while traveling across the state visiting colleges and universities in behalf of the project. All the interns have become close and important friends.

Encouraged by the complete support of Speaker Matt Ryan, we worked on the project relying on the advice and counsel of several other good friends, including legislative historian and author of several Pennsylvania histories, Paul B. Beers. Other prominent and valued advisors were Craig W. Horle, Ph.D. and Jose Foster, Ph.D., primary writers and editors of a series of definitive texts: <u>Lawmaking and Legislators in Pennsylvania, A Biographical Dictionary Vols. I and II</u>, and several other important histories.

Research was completed using the collections of The State Library, The Historical Society of Pennsylvania, the Pennsylvania Historical and Museum Commission, the Free Library of Philadelphia and the State Archives. Hundreds of newspapers across the state were read and re-read in the reading rooms of several libraries and on the Internet.

Christine Goldbeck, of the Speaker's Office, did some stellar proof-reading and editing, as did Norah Griffiths and Rose Kazimierowski.

We appreciate the energetic support of the project supplied by the executive directors of the Bi-partisan Management Committee, Susan Silver Cohen and Peter C. Wambach II.

Artist and illustrator Marsha Wise Conley did her usual great job in the design and layout of the book.

Therese Mitchell, Director of House Republican Communications was our cheerleader and always helpful.

Finally, we extend our most sincere gratitude to the 28 women currently serving in the House. Most took the time to complete an extensive survey, which was used in the preparation of their biographies. I admire them all, but particularly Elinor Taylor, the highly-respected "grande dame" of the House.

ntroduction

The dawn of the 21st century is an exciting and promising time to be a woman interested in political office in Pennsylvania. This was not always so. In the past, women were considered the faceless, forgotten figures in politics. In fact, in Pennsylvania, over 11,000 men have been elected to serve in the House of Representatives since 1682, and only 105 women.

Only since the passage of the 19th Amendment, or the Susan B. Anthony Amendment, of the U. S. Constitution, on August 26, 1920, and beginning with the 1922 elections, women have had the right to be elected to the House. Today, in the Pennsylvania General Assembly of the first months of the new millennium, 28 women are elected members.

A woman running for the Pennsylvania House the last century had to square off against an opponent as tough as any of her likely rivals - - over three centuries of history. This history includes the fact that Pennsylvania has never elected a woman to the United States Senate, or to the offices of governor, lieutenant governor or attorney general. Also, there have been only five female members of the Pennsylvania delegation in the U.S. Congress. Of those, three replaced husbands who died in office. Former state Senator Melissa Hart currently represents Pennsylvania in the Congress, having been elected in November of 2000. She is the first Republican woman in history to be elected to represent Pennsylvania.

1

In Pennsylvania, women make up 52 percent of the population, yet the 5 women serving as senators and 28 female House members represent just over 13 percent of the positions in the state's General Assembly. Only six states are worse in percentage of women elected to their General Assemblies. They include: Arkansas, Mississippi, Kentucky, Oklahoma, South Carolina and Alabama.

In the year 2001, State Treasurer Barbara Hafer is the only woman serving in a statewide executive office in Pennsylvania.

"Politics is very rough," Hafer said. "Anyone can attack you or your family personally. I think women are not choosing politics. I think they are turned off to it generally."

To end the "drought" of women candidates, Republicans like Majority Leader John M. Perzel and Appropriations Chairman John Barley have said they are making serious efforts to recruit women candidates for statewide and legislative offices. These efforts resulted in the election of five new Republican women to the House in the November 2000 elections.

Democrats initiated a "WILL" program, "Women in Legislative Leadership." According to state Representative T.J. Rooney, a male Democrat from Northampton, this effort will not have a substantial impact. He thinks that politics is behind the effort for gender equality in government. Rooney states, "Women candidates can win for us where male candidates sometimes can't: in suburban districts like Montgomery County, the Lehigh Valley, and Pittsburgh suburbs like Butler County. Those are the soccer mom areas, and those are areas where we will recruit and support more women candidates."

Following the 2000 elections, Rooney said that "women make appealing candidates... both major parties are continually looking for women to run for election."

Former House member and now state Senator Lisa Boscola said "older women have told her they grew up in a Pennsylvania where women were told they could only be teachers, nurses or nuns. But that's changing as more and more women go to college and run their own businesses," she said.

The biggest problem for women running for state office in Pennsylvania, suggests newspaper reporter David La Torre, "might be the job itself. With salaries of $61,890, members of Pennsylvania's General Assembly are the third-highest paid in the nation, behind New York and California. Each lawmaker also has a substantial benefits package and list of perks which, among other things, requires taxpayers to pick up the cost for the leasing of automobiles. Some lawmakers have used that perk to drive luxury cars such as Cadillacs or Lincolns."

In response, Senator Boscola replied, "it's always going to be more competitive in a state like this for women, compared to another state that has a part-time legislature and less benefits… so you're always going to have men wanting this job."

Stephen Drachler, spokesman for House Majority Leader Perzel, said the attempt to recruit women was one of the cornerstones of the GOP's effort in 2000. Like Rooney, Drachler said he thinks women resonate with voters on family-related issues.

Former U.S. Democratic Congresswoman Marjorie Margolies-Mezvinsky of Montgomery County, the current head of the Women's Campaign Fund, believes a "women recruitment" process is, in reality, much harder than it sounds. She has said that women face more obstacles than men when campaigning for political office.

3

Margolies-Mezvinsky explains that women are confronted with the issue of family; specifically, raising children. In addition, it is hard for women to break into the "old boy's club of politics," regardless of the political party, county committee, businessmen's group, or labor union. This is why, according to Margolies-Mezvinski, women have begun to organize their own clubs.

Women's organizations have sometimes been successful in accomplishing their objectives, and other times, they have not. Many of the objectives of women's political organizations are as diverse as those of men, yet most women's organizations share certain basic similarities. They exist for the following reasons: to increase women's knowledge of the political process and public policy issues; to increase the involvement of women in politics; to develop cooperation between men and women in government; and to ensure that the state legislature and executive offices are occupied by a number of women that reflects Pennsylvania's actual female population.

Many women who wish to become more involved in politics feel it is necessary to unite. Contrary to the assumption one may be inclined to make from Margolies-Mezvinski's remarks, this is not a new phenomenon. Women have been organizing their own clubs since the first half of the 19th century at the start of the suffrage movement. Since women were granted the right to vote in 1920, they have continued to organize their own clubs, ensuring that this right is protected and strengthened to allow them equal access to the institutions of government. To better understand these goals, one must examine the history of the movement that inspired them.

History of National Women's Suffrage

Before the election in 1922 of the first eight women to serve in the House, women fought long and hard *first*, for the right to vote. It took seven decades of concerted effort for Pennsylvania's and the nation's women to win that right.

They began in 1787 when the U.S. Constitution placed voting qualifications in the hands of the states. Women in all states, except New Jersey, lost the right to vote. In 1807, women lost the right in New Jersey.

The women's movement was tied closely to the abolitionist movement. In the 1830s women formed anti-slavery associations, the forerunners of the suffrage movement. The outspoken leaders of this movement, including Elizabeth Cady Stanton, were banned from speaking publicly against slavery. In 1848, the first Women's Rights convention was held in Seneca Falls, New York. Equal suffrage was proposed by Stanton, and following a debate of so radical a notion, it was adopted.

The Seneca Falls Convention was attended by over 300 people, mostly women, and gatherings such as this were held periodically across the country over the course of the next 20 years. As the article "And Still They Persevered ...A Brief History" suggests, "For many people, these gatherings were the first opportunity to hear women speaking with ease on a public platform, exploring and discussing serious issues with each other, strongly and confidently demanding their rights as women."

When Stanton strode to the speaker's platform at the first-ever women's rights assembly, she thought of the death of her only brother at age 10. Near the casket in their large dark parlor, she climbed onto the knee of her pale, immovable father. At length he heaved a sigh and said, "Oh my daughter, I wish you were a boy." Throwing her arms around his neck, she replied, "I will try to be all my brother was." Later, after she had become the national leader of the suffrage movement, her father questioned her sanity and her husband left town the day of her famous speech at Seneca Falls.

As Stanton raised seven children, she wrote the speeches delivered by her close friend of 50 years, Susan Brownell Anthony, who traveled the country in support of women's rights.

During the Civil War, women put aside suffrage activities to help the war effort.

It was after the war that the right to vote became an even greater concern of women's rights leaders. They were disappointed when the 14th and 15th Amendments neglected to offer women the same voting rights as those of black men.

In 1868, ratification of the 14th Amendment sparked debate over the definitions of "citizenship" and "voters." These terms were defined as "male" and began to raise the question of whether or not women were considered citizens of the United States at all.

A student of history cannot separate women's organizations from the suffrage movement in which they were involved. Knowledge of the movement is knowledge of the history and purpose behind certain women's organizations.

Two women's suffrage organizations were founded in 1869. Each held a different view on both the 15th Amendment and how best to promote suffrage.

The National Woman Suffrage Association (NWSA) was headed by Stanton and Anthony. It opposed the 15th Amendment, which gave the right to vote to black men, on the grounds that it would make it more difficult for women to be granted the right to vote. This organization hoped to accomplish the enfranchisement of women through federal action. However, NWSA's refusal to work for the ratification of the 15th Amendment, in favor of a 16th Amendment that provided universal suffrage, provoked Frederick Douglass to break his ties with both Stanton and Anthony.

The American Woman Suffrage Association (AWSA) was led by Lucy Stone, her husband Harry Blackwell, Julia Ward Howe, Mary Livermore, Henry Ward Beecher, and others. Unlike the NWSA, it was not led exclusively by women and hoped to win support for women's suffrage at the grassroots level. AWSA members formed state-level organizations and published The Woman's Journal to serve as their mouthpiece. The intent of AWSA was to make its proposals for reform seem less radical, even mainstream. The article "A Brief History" quotes from Eleanor Flexner's book Century of Struggle to better detail the mission of AWSA:

The AWSA believed that [the vote] could be won only by avoiding issues that were irrelevant and calculated to alienate the support of influential sections of the community. Its' leaders had no interest in organizing working women, in criticizing churches, or in the divorce question, certainly as matters of public discussion. While paying only lip service to the principle of a

Federal Woman's Suffrage Amendment, they concentrated their practical work for the franchise within several states.

The belief of AWSA was that if enough people from different states could be persuaded to support the cause, a majority of states would make possible what the federal government would not.

Regardless of the efforts of NWSA, the proposed 16th Amendment was rejected. This led suffragists in both organizations to explore other means of achieving enfranchisement. Many contemplated challenging their exclusion in the courts.

Then, in 1867, the 14th Amendment to the U.S. Constitution was passed by Congress, defining citizens as "male." This is the first use of the word male in the Constitution. The same year, equal suffrage became a statewide controversy in the state of Kansas, with its legislature submitting an amendment to the electorate to enfranchise white women, making Kansas the first state in the Union to consider women's suffrage. The women's amendment ultimately was defeated.

In 1868 the 14th Amendment was ratified, giving the right to vote to black men. Women petitioned to be included but were turned down. The same year the New England Suffrage Association was formed and in New Jersey, 172 women attempted to vote, but their ballots were ignored.

Victoria Woodhull argued before Congress in 1871 that women were citizens, therefore their right to vote was protected by the Constitution. Also in that year, a decade before becoming a Philadelphia lawyer, Carrie S. Burnham tried to vote. She took her fight all the way to the state Supreme Court on April 4, 1873, when she argued that as a taxpayer and freeman (she had been assessed and paid her county taxes) she was qualified to vote.

Burnham cited a draft of the Constitution from 1790, Article III, Section I. According to the phrasing of this draft, women had the right to vote. She quoted, "In elections by the citizens, every freeman of the age of 21 years, having resided in the state two years next before the days of election respectively, and paid taxes within that time, shall enjoy the rights of an elector."

The use of the word "man," Burnham argued, in the word "freeman" meant a *human being,* not the gender of a human being. A freeman, she wrote, is the opposite of a slave and "is a compound word, composed of two simple words, "FREI," free or true, and "MANN," a human being, and in accordance with the peculiarity of the German compound words, it emphatically expresses the ideas embodied in the two simple words. It does not mean a free man or a free woman, but a free human being."

Also in 1871, Anthony and 14 other women registered to vote. The following day, 40 other females followed in their footsteps. On election day, 15 of those women, including Anthony, succeeded in voting. Anthony was then arrested, charged and found guilty of "knowingly, wrongfully and unlawfully voting for a representative of the Congress of the United States." She was ordered to pay a fine of $100. In response she said, "May it please your honor, I will never pay a dollar of your unjust penalty." The fine remains unpaid to this day.

Men had several reasons for fighting against women's suffrage. "Women will be coarsened and hardened if they engaged in politics and went to the polls," a railroad president exclaimed as a delegate to the 1873 Constitutional Convention, where suffrage was rejected by a 67-22 vote.

Other men argued that the "frailty of women" made them unsuited to vote. Women's physical weakness was considered potentially dangerous. One man wrote that once a woman arrived at the polls "she would have to mingle among the crowds of men who gather around the polls... and to press her way through them to the ballot box. Assuming she reached the polling place, she might get caught in a brawl and given women's natural fragility, she would be the one to get hurt."

Beyond these reasons existed the belief that allowing women to vote would jeopardize the nation's security and ultimately lead to war. "Allowing women to vote," said convinced anti-suffragists, "would lead to foreign aggression and war." Some men also believed if women got the right to vote they would vote more than once. "Women could hide extra ballots in their voluminous sleeves and slip them quickly into the ballot at once."

In 1875, the U.S. Supreme Court ruled unanimously that citizenship did not necessarily guarantee the right to vote. The court felt the issue of women's suffrage should be decided by the states. Meanwhile, many western states were granting women the right to vote. Sometimes these states battled Congress for their right to do so. In 1869, Wyoming, while still a territory, adopted women's suffrage.

Congress was not intent on approving its application for Wyoming's statehood because it was too progressive with women. However, the state's legislature held fast, declaring, "We will remain out of the union a hundred years rather than come in without the women." Eventually, Wyoming was admitted into the union with its suffrage provision intact. Utah enacted women's suffrage as a territory in 1870 and also entered into the union with suffrage rights for women. Colorado (1893) and Idaho (1896) were other pioneering suffrage states.

Two theories have been suggested to explain why women were granted the right to vote in western states. One theory is that frontier conditions were so harsh that women had an opportunity to prove their worth and equality with men. In this harsh environment, traditional gender roles no longer applied. Another suggested theory is that politicians in the west held the hope that this region would be civilized if women were granted the right to vote and allowed meaningful involvement in public affairs.

Nevertheless, it was more likely than not that "practical politics" served as the reason behind the willingness of western politicians to enfranchise women. For example, the Mormons in Utah hoped that women would favor them in their struggle with the non-Mormon population of miners, rail workers, prospectors, and cowboys who did not work with women.

In the east, the suffrage movement had gained the support of the Women's Christian Temperance Union. Believing women to be more sympathetic to their cause than most men, the union supported suffrage "as a way of protecting the home, women and children." This alignment, however, gave the suffrage movement a powerful opponent in the liquor industry. NWSA President Carrie Chapman Catt later stated that the liquor industry was "the Invisible Enemy," able to manipulate the political system to long delay female enfranchisement.

Through the ensuing years until its ratification, suffragettes demonstrated for the 19th amendment, sometimes incurring the wrath of the local police. Several women were jailed and even more, like Anthony, were fined. Finally, in 1878, the women's suffrage amendment was introduced in the U.S. Congress. In 1884 the U.S House of Representatives debated the issue.

The absence of a national consensus on the suffrage amendment did not stop selected states from electing women. In 1894, three women – the nation's first - were elected to serve in the Colorado House of Representatives and were sworn in January of 1895.

Five years prior to that event, in 1890, having long been separated by their conflicting visions of the movement's goals and the best ways to achieve these goals, AWSA and NWSA placed aside their differences and again united. The new organization became the National American Woman Suffrage Association (NAWSA). Stanton was elected president and Anthony was vice president (she began her tenure as president in 1892).

The organization still desired a federal constitutional amendment that would grant universal suffrage. However, NAWSA leaders agreed that grassroots support must first be obtained within individual states. They believed that if enough of the voters in individual states were persuaded to support suffrage, it would be easier to obtain the three-fourths of the states necessary to ratify the amendment. The new organization decided that the best way to attract support was to avoid radical causes.

The NAWSA knew that many white men in the south were extremely upset that black men had been granted the right to vote and that it was relatively easy for immigrants to gain this right as well. These landmark events made universal suffrage a notion repugnant to many southern men. The NAWSA believed that it needed the support of southern states in order to achieve national suffrage for women, so its leaders began to argue to southern leaders that women's suffrage would not endanger white supremacy in the south but actually help restore it.

They suggested that while women were educated enough and had the proper qualifications that would allow them to vote, black women would be disqualified. White women voting along with white men could override the influence of black male voters and restore white supremacy. If white supremacy could be restored without disenfranchising black men, they argued, the South would not be risking congressional discipline.

Abolitionist Douglas was asked to stay away from the women's rights movement in the south. However, despite these less than conscionable methods, southern leaders made it clear in 1903 that they would not use women to maintain supremacy. Instead, they would simply search for other means of maintaining white supremacy, which, in the words of one Mississippi politician, did not involve "cowering behind petticoats" and destroying the traditional role of women. Yet despite the fact that white suffragists turned their backs on blacks in the late 19th and early 20th centuries, black women remained committed to the suffrage movement.

In addition to the continued support of black women, NAWSA, under Catt's leadership (1900-1904), began to recruit socially prominent women and younger, college-educated women. The movement was influenced by the new ideas of such energetic young leaders as Maud Wood Park and Inez Haynes who formed the College Equal Suffrage League. New tactics introduced by the youthful leaders breathed life into the sagging movement. Such tactics included open-air meetings, parades, and the publishing of literature designated for distribution in schools and libraries. NAWSA sponsored debates and began perfecting a new, less radical image of the movement's own history "in which Anthony was virtually canonized."

In the early 1900s, the nation lost its most prominent suffrage activists. Stanton and Anthony died. Even after her death, Stanton's public image eroded, as the more prim and acceptable Anthony was elevated to represent the suffrage struggle. But Stanton, the fiercer half of the partnership, was clearly the matriarch of the women's movement. Passionately aware of the inequities, insistent and eloquent, she persevered. As Anthony put it, "Cautious, careful people… never can bring about reform. Those who are really in earnest must be willing to… avow their sympathy with despised and persecuted ideas… and bear the consequences."

According to historian Kate Gurnett, no one was more eloquent than Stanton in describing the inequalities of women and more insistent on correcting them.

Stanton's daughter, Harriet Stanton Blatch, took up the torch and formed the Equality League of Self Supporting Women, which became the Women's Political Union in 1910. She introduced the British suffragists' tactics of parades, street speakers and pickets.

Until 1910, there was little success for the movement. No additional pro-suffrage states had been added to the union and the proposed federal amendment did not seem close to passage. In the words of the article "A Brief History," "Interest and enthusiasm were at an all-time low."

However, starting in 1910, more western states adopted suffrage rights for women. They included Washington (1910), California (1911), Oregon (1912), Kansas (1912), and Arizona (1912). Throughout the United States, men and women who supported progressive reforms such as pure food and drug legislation, protection for workers, an end to child labor, and political reform initiatives realized that if women had the right to vote, these measures could be secured.

In 1912, activist Alice Paul returned to the United States from England where she was inspired by many of the tactics of British suffragists. Paul encouraged NAWSA to focus solely on achieving

14

a federal amendment granting suffrage, rather than achieving it through state action alone. Before adopting this strategy, NAWSA parted company with Paul and her followers. It eventually put this idea into effect; however, it refused to implement any of Paul's other methods.

In 1912, Teddy Roosevelt's Progressive Party included women's suffrage in its platform. The following year, Paul was responsible for organizing a parade of over 5,000 women which was held the day Wilson arrived in Washington for his first presidential inauguration ceremony. Few were at the train station to greet Wilson. Instead, the crowds were on Pennsylvania Avenue watching the suffragists. The women's parade was attacked by a mob. Hundreds of women were injured; however, no arrests were made.

In 1915, four states, including Pennsylvania, voted on women's suffrage. All of the campaigns went down "to heartbreaking defeat."

Catt returned to NAWSA as president in late 1915 and adopted a "winning plan" that encouraged NAWSA to continue its work with individual states, never losing sight of the federal amendment as their ultimate goal. Catt asked women in states where suffrage did not exist but was likely to exist to push for a suffrage movement as soon as possible. She asked women in states where defeat was likely, to work for partial suffrage. She asked women in states that already allowed suffrage to pressure their U.S. representatives to support the federal amendment.

Paul and her followers mobilized women voters in western states against President Woodrow Wilson's re-election in 1916. She and her followers also picketed the White House, burning his war-time speeches which praised democracy.

Beginning in January of 1917, the National Women's Party posted silent "Sentinels of Liberty" at the White House. By June, arrests began and nearly 500 women were arrested. Of those, 168 women served jail time and some were brutalized by their jailers. All were released by the following year and an appellate court ruled that the arrests were illegal. President Wilson then declared support for suffrage and the amendment was passed in the U.S. House with exactly a 2/3rds vote, but lost by two votes in the U.S. Senate.

Meanwhile, Catt and others worked to lobby President Wilson and members of congress. When the United States entered World War I, Catt, a pacifist, urged suffragists to support the war effort in order to enhance the patriotic image of women and their movement with powerful politicians. The strategy worked, especially with Wilson, who became a strong advocate of women's suffrage. Congress approved the 19th Amendment and submitted it to the states in June of 1919. Pennsylvania ratified the 19th Amendment on June 24, 1919. It was the seventh state to do so.

There has always been debate among historians whether or not it was Catt, Paul, or both who contributed to the victory of the 19th Amendment in congress. Marjorie Spruill Wheeler states, "…clearly Catt's careful coordination of suffragists all over the nation and skillful political maneuvering, together with the pressure of Wilson and members of congress that Paul and her followers applied by less orthodox methods of persuasion, were all major factors." The writers of "A Brief History," however, lean more in support of the notion that Paul was responsible for creating the conditions that forced a federal amendment:

The NAWSA disapproved of these activities and took great pains to disassociate itself from the National

Woman's Party. Nevertheless, the arrests brought embarrassment to Wilson's administration and publicity to the suffrage cause. They are thought by many to be responsible for increased Congressional activity regarding the federal amendment.

In January of 1919, members of the National Women's Party lighted a guarded "Watchfire for Freedom" which was maintained until after the Suffrage Amendment passed the U.S. Senate on June 4. On that date the battle for ratification by at least 36 states began. Over 14 months later, it became law.

Thirty-six states had to ratify the amendment before it could become a part of the Constitution. By the summer of 1920, only one more state was needed.

President Wilson successfully pressured the reluctant governor of Tennessee to call a special legislative session. Tennessee ratified the amendment on August 18, 1920 due to one 24-year old legislator named Harry Burn, who changed his vote at the insistence of his elderly mother. After anti-Suffragists tried to flee the state in order to avoid a quorum, the vote was reaffirmed for ratification. The 19th Amendment was officially added to the U.S. Constitution on August 26, 1920.

The road to the right to vote was difficult and long, across the country and here in Pennsylvania. A Wilkes-Barre woman, at a celebration of the 75th anniversary of women's suffrage, said in retrospect, "the lack of voting rights early this century was an incredible insult to half of humanity. To think that one sex could vote and one 'didn't have' the mentality or the intelligence or the concern for the country… is more than ridiculous. It's an abomination."

17

Pennsylvania's Early Women Suffragists

In her paper "Philadelphia County Woman Suffrage Society" Liliane S. Howard offers proof of a positive public perception of one suffrage organization's efforts in Philadelphia.

A volunteer group of about 20 men and women organized to hold outdoor meetings that were aimed toward attracting a wider audience of supporters, which included men. This group decided to venture into the streets, meeting men on their ground. No advance notice was given. They traveled to where the crowds gathered: intersections, the entrance to the park, and factory districts. They did not neglect black and immigrant neighborhoods.

Howard describes first-hand that when the women spoke, the crowds flocked, but when men spoke in favor of suffrage, the crowds would disperse. When another woman would take up the theme, the crowd again became attracted. In her paper Howard cites, "It was not that the man made a less interesting talk, but because the man was old stuff. The novelty of women speakers drew them. The intelligence, the fund of information, the logic of their arguments held attention, their dignity was impressive. Questions were sometimes asked, but never was anything discourteous said or done."

Howard further describes that there was no heckling, violence, or "hoodlumism" directed towards the women in Philadelphia. She believes this was due to the dignity of the women in appearance, demeanor and presentation of message.

18

However, despite the account given by Howard, it cannot be overlooked that throughout his term as president, the anti-Wilson banners of suffragists did manage to attract the hostility of onlookers, and violence ensued against female pickets. Many women in fact were arrested, held illegally, and treated roughly in prison.

The women whose short biographies follow were originally from Pennsylvania and were well-known for their work on behalf of women's rights.

Anna Elizabeth Dickinson

Anna Elizabeth Dickinson, of Philadelphia, lived from 1842 to 1932. She was a Quaker who worked as a copyist and teacher. She also worked at the U.S. Mint. Dickinson was a prominent lecturer on the subject of women's rights. She averaged about 150 lectures per season in the late 1860's. Dickinson was as much a champion of the rights of blacks as she was of women's rights.

Despite her public concern for women's rights and her friendships with Stanton and Anthony, Dickinson was considered "aloof from" the suffrage movement.

Later in her life, Dickinson was an actress and a playwright who played a female Hamlet in 1882. In 1891, she was committed to Danville Hospital for the Insane, but later was released and won damages. Sadly, Dickinson died in obscurity.

Lavinia Lloyd Dock

Lavinia Lloyd Dock, of Harrisburg, was born in 1858. She was a graduate of Bellevue Hospital and became a settlement house nurse in New York. Dock helped to professionalize nursing. She was a contributing editor to the American Journal of Nursing and, in 1890, she compiled the first and said to be one of the "long most important" nursing manuals on drugs, Materia

Medica for Nurses. She also wrote most of A History of Nursing (2 vols., 1907; 2 more vols., 1912; later revised and abridged). Dock was arrested for attempting to vote in New York in 1896. However, jail time was refused to her by then-police commissioner Theodore Roosevelt. At the age of 54, Dock hiked 13 days to Albany in support of suffrage. She also served on Paul's Advisory Council and led the first group of pickets to the White House. Dock was jailed three times for her involvement with the cause of women's suffrage.

She gave up nursing as a practice at the age of 50 and remained dedicated to activism on the controversial social issues of her time. Dock was an ardent campaigner against venereal disease and prostitution. She was "never one to avoid unpopular positions" and proved this by speaking out against World War I and advocating birth control. Dock died on April 17, 1956.

Florence Kelley

Florence Kelley, of Philadelphia, was a social reformer strongly influenced by the Quakers. She graduated from Cornell University in 1882 but was denied entrance to the University of Pennsylvania law school because she was a woman. Instead, Kelley studied at the University of Zurich, Switzerland while teaching.

In Switzerland, Kelley became a socialist and translated Friedrich Engel's Condition of the Working Class in England. She married a Russian medical student and had three children. Upon their arrival in the United States, she and her husband separated. They divorced in 1891.

Kelley joined Hull House and spent much of her effort calling attention to the working conditions of women and children.[54] She fought for the minimum wage and an end to child labor. While surveying city slums and inspecting sweatshops, she risked exposure to smallpox. An assassination attempt was even made on Kelley's life.

By taking night classes, Kelley received her law degree at Northwestern in 1894. In 1899, she became the general secretary of the new National Consumer's League. Moving to New York City, Kelley wrote a book titled <u>Some Ethical Gains Through Legislation</u> (1905). In 1909, she helped to form the National Association for the Advancement of Colored People. In 1919, Kelley helped to form the Women's International League for Peace and Freedom. After World War I, she worked so hard in her efforts to continue promoting child labor legislation that she was branded a communist.

Frances Perkins described Kelley in the following way: "explosive, hot-tempered, determined, she was no gentle saint." Kelley died on February 17, 1932.

Jane Grey Cannon Swisshelm

Jane Grey Cannon Swisshelm was born in 1815. She was originally from Pittsburgh. Swisshelm was a "passionate anti-slavery journalist." She taught, painted, and made corsets while editing various Minnesota newspapers.

Swisshelm was a nurse during the Civil War and lectured and wrote articles on women's rights. In 1872, Swisshelm toured Illinois in support of suffrage. She died on July 22, 1884.

Cornelia Bryce Pinchot

Cornelia Bryce Pinchot was born in Newport, Rhode Island in 1881. She was educated in private schools and traveled frequently with her parents throughout Europe. She was reputed to be spirited and independent. Her friend, Theodore Roosevelt, described her political mind as one of the keenest he had ever known.

Pinchot was an attractive woman who dressed in flamboyant clothes and dyed her hair red. A Progressive, she met Gifford Pinchot at a Bull Moose campaign and married him in 1914.

Pinchot's political interests were sparked by the issue of women's suffrage. However, she spoke in support of birth control and educational reform. She attacked sweatshops and was a pacifist who worked for the Red Cross during World War I. Pinchot supported prohibition, saying, "To vote dry is not enough. Public men and women ought to live as they vote."

In 1920, her husband ran for governor of Pennsylvania. Pinchot campaigned with him for honesty in government and "cleaning up the mess in Harrisburg." After his victory, Governor Pinchot declared, "It was due to Mrs. Pinchot and the women she organized, far more than any other single factor, that we won."

In February of 1923, along with Marion Margery Warren Scranton (the mother of Governor William W. Scranton and grandmother to Lieutenant Governor Bill Scranton) and others, Pinchot founded the State Council of Republican Women. The organization began with 37 clubs and 5,935 members. She ran for Congress in 1928, promoting labor law reform but lost the election. In the 1930's, she ran twice for Congress and once for governor. She lost all races. She often was quoted as saying, "Politics is the best of all indoor sports."

Many of Pinchot's remarks and antics were the focus of headlines. In 1933, at the Allentown "Baby Strike" of child-labor protesters, she marched wearing a bright red corduroy coat. People called her a Bolshevik. Also in 1933, she and her husband gave a dinner for Franklin and Eleanor Roosevelt. The cost of the meal was 5 ° cents per plate. The meal consisted of black bean soup, cabbage rolls, and breadsticks. The food had been purchased at a "commissary of the unemployed." One critic called the event "an example of exhibitionism and bad taste … propaganda for radical causes."

Pennsylvania historian Paul Beers believes that "Pinchot's sense of manhood was secure enough for him not to feel threatened by such an outspoken spouse. He agreed with her idealistic view that women's political equality would be a major step toward eliminating male flattery, condescension, and threats as well as female nagging, scolding, and silent awe."

In 1949, Pinchot was on hand at the dedication in Washington state of the Gifford Pinchot National Forest. Later in life, she held numerous diplomatic positions, serving as a delegate to the United Nations Scientific Conference on Conservation and Utilization of Resources in 1949. She also made a number of goodwill visits to Mediterranean countries. Pinchot died in Washington, D.C. in 1960.

In addition to these high-profile women, many other Pennsylvanian women were dedicated to the cause of women's suffrage. After 1920, several united to organize women's organizations and clubs dedicated to the preservation of the right to vote and strengthening women's involvement in the formation of policy.

# istory of Pennsylvania's Statewide Women's Political Organizations

Pennsylvania State Council of Republican Women

The Pennsylvania State Council of Republican Woman was organized in late February, 1923. As a group, it supported women legislative candidates. At its first meeting, "various organizations were asked to present their legislative programs." The groups included the Consumer's League, Woman's Trade Union League, State Federation of Women's Clubs, Women's Christian Temperance Union and Farm Woman.

The Council's by-laws were adopted at the February meeting and Article II listed the objectives of the Council. The objectives included: to serve as a clearing house for Republican Women's activities and to provide a center for political education, legislative information and practical services; to increase the number of women registered and enrolled in the Republican party and unite their efforts along party lines; and, to secure equal representation for women with men on state and county committees within the party throughout the state.

In November of 1923, the first annual convention of the Pennsylvania State Council of Republican Women was held at the

24

Penn Harris Hotel in Harrisburg. On day two of the three-day series of events, Representative Alice M. Bentley was the featured speaker in a session held in the House of Representatives. The title of her presentation was "Impressions of a Woman Legislator."

The minutes of the convention, which can be reviewed today at the Harrisburg office of the Pennsylvania Council of Republican Women on Second Street, carried the following account of Bentley's speech:

> *"Miss Bentley humorously described the experience of running for office and serving in the legislature. Out of the 50 (there actually were only 38) women candidates for the Assembly in Pennsylvania eight women were elected. She is proud of the record of Crawford County. In 1921, a woman was elected for Jury Commissioner, in 1922 women were elected to the county committee, and in 1923 a woman was elected to the legislature. Several minor Court House offices were also filled by women. No woman who has run for office in Crawford County has been defeated."*

Later the same morning, and in the Senate Chamber, Representative Gertrude MacKinney presided over a discussion of "Legislation and Enforcement." The minutes carried the following information: "Miss Gertrude MacKinney reported for the Legislative and Law Enforcement group. It was the consensus of opinion of the women assembled in conference on legislation and enforcement that it is a woman's problem to make the 18th Amendment a fact as well as the law."

It continued, "that encouragement be given to agencies engaged in enforcement. That organizations endorsing enforcement should see to it that dry candidates are elected from Town Con-

25

stable to President of the United States. That the Pennsylvania State Council of Republican Women begin at once to secure dry candidates for the primaries."

Usually, national organizations organize branches throughout the states and communities of America. In the case of the Pennsylvania Council of Republican Women the opposite occurred. In 1938, the Pennsylvania Council of Republican Women was instrumental in organizing the National Federation of Republican Women (NFRW). The Governing Board of the NFRW is comprised of all state council presidents and an elected executive committee.

During the 1960's, membership in the Council reached its peak; it had over 400 local councils and over 60,000 members. The Council believes that since the 1970's membership has, in part, decreased because of the diminished amount of spare time available to working women.

Today, the Pennsylvania Council of Republican Women is composed of over 130 local councils and membership totals approximately 10,000. The council's board of directors is comprised of 30 directors who are recommended by a nominating committee and are elected at an annual convention. The board of directors meets four times a year.

The council publishes a newsletter, NEWSLINE. It is issued three times a year and recognizes the accomplishments of the state council, local councils, and particular members. The council publishes various congressional and legislative newsletters which are meant to "[alert] members to legislative issues under discussion."

Although no longer concerned with the enforcement of prohibition, the council is still concerned with the election of all Republican candidates to public office, increasing membership within the Republican party, increasing women's knowledge of public policy issues and party principles, as well as increasing women's involvement in politics.

Current work revolves around efforts to influence welfare reform, education, and efficiency and honesty in government. The council still strives to secure for women equal representation with men on state and county committees within the Republican party and to help women achieve elected office.

The Pennsylvania Federation of Democratic Women

The 1920's also saw the foundation of another political party-affiliated women's organization. In 1927, Emma Guffey Miller, of Slippery Rock, along with a group of other women suffragists, organized the Federation of Democratic Women to "promote the appointment and election of Democratic women to responsible positions within all branches of government, to encourage the advancement of women in both the public and private sectors, and to advocate the principles of the Democratic Party."

Miller, known affectionately as "The Old Gray Mare," was the sister of U.S. Senator Joe Guffey, one of the most disliked political figures of his time. She, on the other hand, was surely "a cherished character in Pennsylvania politics." Both were Democratic National Committee members. Guffey served 20 years and Miller, the first woman elected to the Democratic National Convention, served a record 38 years, from 1932 until 1970. At the first national convention in 1924, she became the first American woman to receive a vote for a presidential nomination.

At the 1964 Democratic National Convention in Atlantic City, Miller stayed in a hotel room next to NBC commentator David Brinkley. As Beers describes, "She was 89. Brinkley was almost half her age and twice her size. After the first night, Brinkley jokingly complained to television viewers that he had been kept awake almost all night by Mrs. Miller's politicking and telephoning. He said he never saw anyone smoke and drink bourbon as she did." Miller battled for women's rights and women candidates. She advocated what she referred to as "sensible liquor laws" and was described as intelligent, energetic, and friendly. She died in 1970 at the age of 95.

For a long time, the Pennsylvania Federation of Democratic Women was a political social group that served as an aid to the Democratic party by assisting in the work of political campaigns. The organization also educated women voters on the political process and policy issues. For the last 20 years, the federation has remained committed to performing these tasks. However, it has become more aggressive in *leading* campaigns for specific candidates and public policy issues.

Since 1979, the organization has operated a political action committee (PAC) which exists for the purpose of raising money for women candidates. The money is used to educate women on how to run for political office and is dispersed after the Democratic primary. During primary elections, the federation does not support particular candidates, but it "actively" supports the nominees and platform of the Democratic Party during the general election. Despite the fact that it gives approximately $15 to $20 thousand annually to women candidates, the federation does not exist merely to raise money — members also assist with petition signings and guiding people to the polls.

Political networking among elected officials and candidates recently has become a primary objective of the organization.

The federation believes that networking among candidates is a way of helping women office seekers strengthen their tickets, especially with other women candidates in the county or legislative district. However, networks also are established among candidates and those who have already been elected to public office. This helps both the candidates and elected officials share, test, and strengthen their policy ideas and campaign strategies.

Today the Federation of Democratic Women has more than 4,000 members. The affiliates of the federation are located throughout the commonwealth. They are grouped into 18 geographic regions, each coordinated by a director. The entire organization is run by a state executive board which consists of a president, six vice-presidents, a treasurer, corresponding and recording secretaries, and committee chairs.

The organization further provides financial assistance in the form of five annual Memorial Scholarships of $750 each to women college students "whose need and dedication to the Democratic principles are noteworthy." Local affiliates recommend the college juniors to receive the grants for their senior year.

Each year the federation also honors an outstanding Democratic woman elected to public office in Pennsylvania. These women have made contributions to the commonwealth and have supported the federation and the Democratic Party. Honorees are additionally recognized for their efforts to help other women who are seeking elected office. Past recipients who served in the state House of Representatives include former state Senator and House member Jeanette F. Reibman, former state Representative Ruth Corman Rudy and current state Representative Linda Bebko-Jones.

Peg Hain, former president of the federation, believes that her group, as well as other women's organizations, have made good strides for women candidates, especially at the local level of government. Serving in local offices gives women the opportunity to gain credibility with the voters and overcome gender stereotypes. This ultimately will allow women to win the higher statewide and legislative offices.

Across the nation, and especially in Pennsylvania, women still have a long way to go in terms of how successfully they are being elected to public office. Hain acknowledges, however, that both male and female views on gender have evolved considerably over the course of several decades. Citing the amount of progress women have made since the 1920's, Hain adds that it must be kept in perspective, "Remember that men have been doing this for over 300 years."

League of Women Voters of Pennsylvania

Upon helping women achieve the right to vote in 1920, delegates from the National American Woman Suffrage Association (NAWSA) created the League of Women Voters (LWV) to ensure that the new right would be protected and developed to allow women further access to the political process long dominated by men. In her convention address, Catt proposed the creation of this new league:

"The League of Women Voters is not to dissolve any present organization but to unite all existing organizations of women who believe in its principles. It is not to create sex antagonism but to develop cooperation between men and women. It is not to lure women from partisanship but to combine them in an effort for legislation which will protect coming movements, which

we cannot even foretell, from suffering the untoward conditions which have hindered for so long the coming of equal suffrage. Are the women of the United States big enough to see their opportunity?"

The first national president of the LWV was Maud Wood Park. Two years prior to her election, she was instrumental in helping to steer the woman's suffrage amendment through congress.

Park and others believed that the education of all citizens should be the primary aim of the league. The goal of the Pennsylvania LWV is to promote an informed, responsible electorate and a responsible government. This is accomplished through efforts to provide citizens with candidate meetings, voter's guides on the candidates and the issues, the opportunity to participate on juries, the opportunity to vote via absentee ballot, and information on voter registration and the voting process. The league also conducts interviews with legislators and offers seminars on public policy and civic-oriented topics.

Since the 1920's, the league has provided millions with the chance to become more informed participants in their government. It does not endorse candidates for political office. The statement of the Pennsylvania LWV from 1920 reads: *"The League of Women Voters is all-partisan; its members are free to join the political party of their choice ... An outside group, nonpartisan, unpartisan and all-partisan, will be able to agitate and educate without fear or favor in behalf of needed changes in our fundamental system."*

In the 1920's, the LWV implemented the following principles as part of its mission statement: legislation in support of collective bargaining, child labor laws, a minimum wage, compulsory education, a joint federal and state merit-based civil service, and

31

equal opportunity for women in government and industry. In Pennsylvania, it worked to abolish the poll tax and the need for a tax receipt as a qualification for voting. It also sought to establish an affidavit of necessity for assistance in voting, instigate a balanced state budgetary system, and revise county tax and assessment laws.

Throughout the 1930's, the LWV worked at the national level to help pass Social Security and food and drug acts. Because of the Depression, many of the league's original goals from the previous decade were adopted, introducing the federal government to social-welfare policy. During the 1930's, the LWV supported a national and state-wide level civil service employment system based on merit rather than a spoils system.

In Pennsylvania, the LWV made attempts to do the following: abolish the fee system for magistrates, aldermen and justices of the peace; improve juvenile court and probation procedures; establish and support laws that removed legal discriminations against married women; revise the state aid to schools to provide a minimum educational standard for all children; establish junior colleges and provide vocational training throughout the state; and consolidate Philadelphia City and County.

The 1940's presented more opportunities for the League of Women Voters of Pennsylvania to attempt its progressive reforms. In the Keystone State, it sought to reapportion the legislature, establish an election system that would promote the choice of competent officials as well as protect the voters against fraud and coercion by political candidates, reorganize county and local governments to ensure that they would be allowed home rule, distribute state aid to schools equally, and create county public health departments.

During the 1950's, at a time when it was extremely dangerous to speak out against the "witch-hunt" practices of the U.S. House Un-American Affairs Committee and U.S. Senator Joseph McCarthy, the LWV studied the infringement of individual liberties and argued against the constitutionality of loyalty oaths. In Pennsylvania, the LWV made efforts to institute the non-partisan election of judges and school board officials, establish home rule for third class cities, consolidate school districts for purposes of efficiency and sound economics, and extend the vote to absentee citizens.

During the 1960's, the League of Women Voters directed its attention to the Civil Rights Movement. It promoted the idea of equal access of all people to education, employment, and housing. Local LWVs spoke in favor of fair housing, a greater housing supply for low-income families, and racial balance in schools. In Pennsylvania, the LWV began increasing the use of the voting machine.

Since the nation's Watergate crisis, the league has been recommitted to its belief in the need for government accountability at all levels, government accessibility, and awareness of the rights of its citizens. It is the goal of the LWV to abolish public distrust and hostility towards the political process by advocating changes in that process, i.e. campaign finance reform. It continues to provide opportunities for public discussion and stresses the need for our government to be more representative of the many segments of our nation.

Pennsylvania Commission for Women

What started on June 5, 1964, under Governor William Scranton as the Commission on the Status of Women has turned into the advisory office on women's issues of today. Following President John F. Kennedy's lead, Scranton created the commission to promote the economic, educational, health and legal rights of women. Governor Milton Shapp officially created the Pennsylvania Commission for Women in 1972.

While the organization focuses on women's issues serving all of Pennsylvania's women, members of the state legislature often have become outspoken about the commission's activities. In 1977, the group, as an advocate for women's reproductive rights, strongly opposed a bill that called for a federal convention to amend the U.S. Constitution to outlaw abortion. But backlash from abortion opponents in the General Assembly resulted in the commission dropping abortion as an issue.

When it was abolished by Governor Tom Ridge in 1996 - - he did not include the Commission in his 1997-98 budget — some lawmakers tried to save the commission by legislating that it be taken out of the Governor's Office and placed under the legislature. "Ridge's budget secretary explained that the women's commission was dropped because its "work has been accomplished."

In response to the Ridge administration's actions, Representative Connie Williams, a Democrat from Montgomery County, who was at the time a newly elected legislator, introduced an amendment to the state budget reinstating the commission and raising its appropriation from $250,000 to $750,000. "Hooray for Connie Williams," a member of the commission wrote, adding that the $250,000 appropriation amounted to just four cents per Pennsylvania woman.

One year after he cut the funding, Governor Ridge reversed himself by including $250,000 to recreate the commission in 1997-98.

Since its re-establishment in June of 1997, the commission has been under the jurisdiction of Governor Ridge's Executive

Offices. It consists of three employed staff members and 17 appointed commissioners representing different parts of the state. Commissioners serve two-year terms. Members serve on one of six committees: communication, information and marketing, partnerships and collaboration, economic development, safe day care/healthcare, and legislative issues and budget. Commissioners represent a cross-section of Pennsylvania's citizens in terms of geography, ethnicity, race, economic background, and age.

In October of 1998, commissioners voted unanimously to focus on three issues: child care, economic self-sufficiency for women, and family violence prevention. Since the 1970's, the commission has been concerned with the eradication of sex discrimination. In a 1975 edition of its publication <u>News</u>, the commission stated, "Though lacking enforcement power, the commission has been charged with the responsibility of planning and implementing programs to ensure that women in Pennsylvania are equal participants in the life of the commonwealth."

Today, the Pennsylvania Commission for Women continues to make policy recommendations to the governor and the appropriate agencies. These recommendations are based on current studies and hearings in areas of women's interest. The commission also sponsors educational seminars throughout the state. It provides a professional speakers bureau and serves as a link to the governor for individuals and other women's organizations. Basically, the commission serves as a "resource center" equipped with the means to refer women with "discrimination, harassment, or other complaints, questions about programs, funding resources, business opportunities and other concerns to the source of appropriate assistance."

In August of 1999, the commission published a directory for women and their families which lists women's organizations and state services in the fields of education, health, housing, the arts, family planning, child care, etc. In the words of the commission, these directories provide Pennsylvanians with "necessary and useful information that may assist in the development of partnerships and establish a network with the various state-wide women's organizations. By developing a network for women's issues, the women in Pennsylvania will be able to present a united voice in communities and across the Commonwealth."

Through the years, various female members of the state legislature have served on the Pennsylvania Commission for Women. These women include: Representative Patricia Crawford (1975-77), Senator Jeanette F. Reibman (1975-94), Representative Rita Clark (1979-82), Representative Ruth Corman Rudy (1989-90), Representative Linda Bebko-Jones (1989-90), Representative Connie R. Maine (1991-92), and Representative Phyllis Mundy (1993-96).

Distinguished Daughters of Pennsylvania

Every year, a limited number of Pennsylvanian women are honored as Distinguished Daughters of Pennsylvania at the Governor's Residence. The governor and first lady present the recipients with medals and citations. The ceremony is organized by Distinguished Daughters and the Pennsylvania Commission for Women.

The idea of honoring women for their achievements came into being in October of 1948. At that time, Governor James H. Duff was planning a "Pennsylvania Week" to promote the state and its achievements. Women suggested that outstanding Pennsylvanian women be recognized for their achievements as well, and Duff agreed. From that day in 1948, the Distinguished Daughters has made it the purpose of its existence to recognize professional and volunteer women.

For accepting nominations, the Distinguished Daughters is divided into three regions: eastern, central, and western. An area chair administers each region. The organization also has a president, a vice-president, a secretary, and a treasurer. These officers are elected to administer the entire organization.

Women are proposed to receive the honors of the Distinguished Daughters by "civic, cultural, professional, and institutional" organizations throughout the state. Their accomplishments must be of state-wide or national importance. The nominees do not need to be native Pennsylvanians; however, they must be residents of the state. Nominees are reviewed by the regional boards of Distinguished Daughters. The names of selected nominees are forwarded to the state organization. A meeting in Harrisburg is held to decide the final selections, all Distinguished Daughters are invited. The governor's office notifies the recipients.

As of 2000, 381 women have been recognized as Distinguished Daughters of Pennsylvania. The following female members of the Pennsylvania House of Representatives received the honor through the decades: Ruth Grigg Horting (1957), Marian E. Markley (1957), Mary A. Varallo (1959), Mary Thompson Denman (1965), Jeanette F. Reibman (1968), and Helen Dickerson Wise (1998).

Pennsylvania Women's Campaign Fund

When the Pennsylvania Women's Campaign Fund, or PWCF, was founded in 1982, women held only four percent of the seats in the General Assembly. The PWCF exists solely for the purpose of raising funds for "progressive women candidates of both political parties, with a focus on the state legislature."

According to its bylaws, to qualify for financial assistance from the PWCF women candidates must be of "progressive opinion" on a variety of public policy issues. These positions should include "overt support" for the following: the full implementation of the state Equal Rights Amendment; equality in the quality of educational opportunity and availability of resources; "comprehensive family planning and reproductive services accessible to all women, including services for curtailing unwanted or medically inadvisable pregnancies;" services for victims of domestic violence, rape or incest; improved access to social services for women in need, such as poor women, elderly women and teen mothers; affirmative action; increased employment opportunity; and efforts to eliminate sexual harassment.

Women candidates also must have shown "a demonstrated understanding that most problems of women impact more severely on minority women."

PWCF is a multi-partisan organization. For example, in the 1992 general election four new members of the state House of Representatives were women. All ran for open seats and won in part due to the help of PWCF. Two women, Representatives Kathy Manderino, of Philadelphia County, and Linda Bebko-Jones, of Erie County, were Democrats and two women, Representatives Lita Indzel Cohen, of Montgomery County, and Representative Carole Rubley, of Luzerne County, were Republicans.

In the organization's Spring 1993 newsletter, Cohen said of the PWCF, "The Pennsylvania Women's Campaign Fund provided support and resources throughout my campaign. I appreciated knowing that the organization was there for me. I am glad to know that the PWCF helps other women candidates have that confidence as well."

The organization is a non-profit corporation with a registered PAC. It is funded solely through voluntary contributions from individuals and organizations. Pennsylvania Women's Campaign Fund works closely with the National Women's Campaign Fund.

In a state that ranks near the bottom in the nation in terms of how many women representatives are in the legislature, organizations like PWCF are justified in believing they are needed. This belief is best summarized by Democratic Representative Phyllis Mundy, in her statement to the same spring edition of <u>Pennsylvania Women's Campaign Fund News</u>, "The Pennsylvania Women's Campaign Fund helps women candidates achieve their goals, and in doing so improves our state's political climate."

More Women Candidates

More Women Candidates is a non-partisan organization designed to educate women about the operation of state and local government and the skills needed by a candidate running for office. The organization encourages women to run for public office and encourages political parties to seek women as candidates. The organization does not support any particular party, candidate, philosophy, or cause.

More Women Candidates was established in 1981 by the Pennsylvania Commission for Women and other female leaders of state-wide women's organizations. It develops and provides communities with courses on women in politics and seeks the funds necessary to expand the educational opportunities of all women in Pennsylvania.

Pennsylvania Elected Women's Association

Founded in April of 1981, the purposes of the nonprofit, nonpartisan organization are to encourage women to seek elective office, to educate women about governmental problems and the political process and to promote their participation in public affairs.

In its bylaws, the group also lists the following purposes and policies: to provide a form for elected women officials to address appropriate issues, to ease cooperation and communications among elected women in Pennsylvania, and to provide an educational clearinghouse for information on governmental problems and women's political participation.

Pennsylvania's First Women Representatives

The 19th Amendment took effect nationally on August 26, 1920. For the first time, women were eligible to run for the House, however, the adoption of the amendment came too late for women to run in the 1920 election.

In the election of 1922, eight of the 38 women seeking House seats in Pennsylvania won. In contrast, in 1923 there were no women in Congress and New York state had 33 women run for its legislature and Congress and all lost their elections. Pennsylvania was followed by Connecticut with seven women legislators, Ohio with six, New Jersey with three and Massachusetts with two.

The Harrisburg newspaper erroneously reported that only seven women were elected to the House following the November 7, 1922 election. The same edition carried a story that reflected the mood in Pennsylvania, although it was about the defeat in Oklahoma of Congressional incumbent Miss Alice M. Robertson. She said, "men want only the women's vote in politics. They don't want women to hold office. My defeat bears that contention out."

"Don't pity me," Robertson urged, and continued, "after all, my defeat has relieved a great burden. Nobody knows how hard it is for women to stand up and pass on questions that confronted me in Congress. It is especially hard for women."

Representative Sarah Gertrude MacKinney, the first woman elected from Butler County, was the highest vote-getter of four candidates - the others were men - from her county, garnering 5,987 votes, 300 more than the nearest opponent. Election day was busy in Butler, with throngs of voters waiting outside the newspaper office and Republican headquarters until well after midnight for returns.

It was reported that "Many women braved the chilly weather to stand in the street and watch the bulletin board. Miss Gertrude MacKinney, Butler's first woman candidate for a state office, took the lead at the start of the returns and kept it."

"Ladies and gentlemen of the General Assembly," was said for the first time on January 2, 1923 by departing Governor William C. Sproul in his welcoming address to the House, which included eight Republican women.

The first Democrat, Anna M. Brancato {later Mrs. Anna Wood} of Philadelphia, did not win election until 1932.

The first eight women legislators were hailed as pioneers and women of courage. They are still admired today. Representative Linda Bebko-Jones, a Democrat from Erie elected in 1992, when asked who she thinks is the most admired woman {women} in Pennsylvania answered, "All the women who were first elected to the Pennsylvania General Assembly in 1922... they broke the ground for all of us who serve now. They gave us the courage to continue their work."

The first women elected, in addition to MacKinney, included: Alice M. Bentley, of Philadelphia; Rosa S. deYoung, of Philadelphia; Sarah McCune Gallagher, Ph.D., of Cambria County; Helen Grimes, of Allegheny County; Lillie H. Pitts, of Philadelphia; Martha G. Speiser, of Philadelphia; and, Martha G. Thomas, of Chester County.

A distinguishing feature of these women was family political connections and political activity by other family members. Speiser's husband, Maurice, in fact had served in the 1913-14 legislature. Their complete biographies are found in the "Past Women Legislators" section of this book.

The Harrisburg Telegraph featured photographs of the eight women spread over four columns.

In his address, Sproul said, "it is historic in the annals of the State in that, for the first time, women citizens of Pennsylvania sit here as members of the legislative body. This is the consummation of the hope that some of us have long entertained."

Then, noting the other legislators, Sproul observed that the new female legislators "will also be beneficial and reflect some glory upon the male members of this particular session and will be remembered in their biographies, also." The press reported that each of the ladies was "almost hidden behind a screen of flowers"

"Delegations of friends from their districts accompanied some of the women when they came to take their seats," the Harrisburg newspaper noted. In the same edition, it was reported that the legislative committee of the Women's Republican Club would "be at the Capitol this morning when the Legislature opens to greet the women legislators." Also, the day before swearing-in, the women legislators were the guests of honor at the annual New Years Day Open House that was held at the Harrisburg Women's Club.

Bentley said, "that the other women were urging her to introduce a resolution asking 'that the men please smoke.'"

Grimes said, "We are going to watch our step and go slowly.

It is not my intention at least to reform anything or anybody."

In a front page story, the <u>Butler Eagle</u> reported that the newly-elected women "are going to prove regular, hard-working, business-like legislators, according to the impression they have created since they were sworn in Tuesday."

"Recent masculine fears that the presence of women might be a hindrance to the expeditious transaction of business in the house have been abandoned already," wrote a reporter, who continued, "At the opening session it was indicated that the women members intend to mix with the men, serve on committees with them, and to work in harmony with them just the same way any other novice members would."

Grimes said it was not her intention to "reform anything or anybody. I hope to get on one of the committees - I don't care which one - and whatever one they give me will receive my utmost attention. I shall plunge in and do my part, whatever that part may be."

The women lawmakers showed a social consciousness during the 1923-24 legislative session. Although never a deliberate "women's bloc," then or since, the pioneers' first bill, introduced by Speiser, abolished solitary confinement in prisons. Their major self-interest accomplishment was to update the Election Law by defining a woman's domicile for voting registration as "determined for all purposes as if she were married."

Although most of the women won election with the help of members of the anti-liquor movement, the eight women were not strict prohibitionists. A stringent "dry-bill" passed the House in 1923, with three women voting against it.

Governor Gifford Pinchot also was elected in 1922. During

his campaign, after the primary, he wrote an article for the September edition of The Ladies Home Journal titled "The Influence of Women in Politics."

"Woman today," he wrote, "exerts a power, not a mere influence in politics - an independent power co-equal with the power of man. She has stepped out of her orchestra seat and become the leading woman in the play."

Pinchot felt that women in politics play an absolutely clean game. That is, "they have brought the highest standards into a contest that has commonly been sullied by shady and evil practices."

In his conclusions about women's role in politics, Pinchot wrote, "the foundation of health and efficiency in all human affairs is honesty and courage, and these are the very qualities which women have brought and will continue to bring into American public life." He also gave credit for his winning the primary to the women who supported his campaign, including his wife (see section on Cornelia Bryce Pinchot).

In his article Pinchot called women "realists" as mothers, and housekeepers "the managing sex." He said they are interested in "moral issues" and law enforcement, and "are equal partners in everything that concerns the state." He concluded, "I am inclined to think they will end by cleaning up the politics of the whole state."

Between 1930 and 1950, a "cult of domesticity" wrapped most women in traditional roles and expectations.

ontemporary Politics

Women today who run for office "must work harder than men, can be expected to be judged more harshly, must exert more effort drumming up money and have to deal with voters and party regulars who don't want anyone bucking the male-dominated status quo."

The 28 women currently serving represent 13.8 percent of the 203-Member House. Yet, women hold a population edge in the state - 52 to 48 percent - according to the Institute of State and Regional Affairs at Penn State.

According to the National Conference of State Legislatures, most states now average 21.8 percent female members in their legislatures. Only six states have a lower percentage of women legislators. Washington state has the most, where 41 percent of legislators are women.

In an October 1999 article about women in elections, reporter Linda Feldman reported "women face many barriers to elective office. They have a harder time than men raising money and, in general, a harder time being taken seriously." She was quoting a study conducted by the Women's Leadership Fund of newspaper coverage of selected 1998 political races.

According to the study, women candidates for office receive on average less newspaper coverage of their positions on issues and more on personal characteristics than do male candidates. "Personal characteristics" include age, marital status, children, personality, appearance and qualifications. Overall, women do retain some advantage over men candidates, according to the polling data. Voters say women candidates "share their values" more than men candidates, have better ideas, and are more tolerant.

Journalists more often include a woman's age, marital status and the number of children she has than they do in stories about male candidates. Reporters also describe the personality and appearance of women more frequently than men.

"In subtle ways, it {a reporter} magnifies stereotypes and makes it harder for the woman to be taken seriously. That means it is not an absolutely level playing field," says Kathleen Hall Jamieson, director of the Annenberg Public Policy Center of the University of Pennsylvania.

"How many girls are told by their parents, 'You're going to grow up to be president,'" asks Bernadette Comfort, administrative director for the Center for Women in Politics in Pennsylvania at Chatham College in Pittsburgh. She adds, "A healthy and thriving democracy only works when we have representative democracy. When women represent 50 percent of the population, but only about 13 percent of the state Legislature {percent includes both House and Senate} I think we have a real problem."

Representative Pat Vance believes that Pennsylvania has such a low ranking because of "the high demands of the legislative career and the amount of campaign funding needed to mount a successful campaign."

In her final remarks in the House Chamber, Representative Patricia Carone, who retired in 1998, said "I would like very much for the leaders on both sides to think about the fact that we have very few women in this chamber and that perhaps together, they could determine how they could look at both of their parties to see of they could not go out and let women recognize that there is a greater place and a greater role for them. We know we are really low on the bottom as far as states go nationwide, and I really think a few more skirts would be a lot of help here, guys."

"Sometimes when there has been a big huddle, like over guns in December of 1993, and I would look over at that huddle and there was not one skirt in the crowd, I would think, ah gee, maybe I should go up and get to be a part of it. I think we can offer you something. However, I think perhaps sometimes you do not understand us on occasion, not all of you," Carone said.

Representative Theresa Forcier (R-Crawford) wrote that the most difficult challenge facing women candidates for public office is "holding your own in a predominately male world."

tatus of Women in 2001

The U.S. Census Bureau reports that among citizens, women were significantly more likely than men to have voted in the 1996 presidential election (60 percent vs. 57 percent). In 1984, women's voting rates in presidential elections surpassed those of men for the first time since the Census Bureau began collecting voting data in 1964.

Nationally, women's voting rates have been higher than men's ever since; however, Pennsylvania ranks 48th of 50 states and the District of Columbia in Women's Composite Political Participation and Representation Index, and 44th in women's voter registration.

An index revealing "women in elected office composite" published in 1998 by George Washington University rated Pennsylvania 46th, again, near the bottom. According to the university findings, Pennsylvania women tend to vote less frequently than in other states. Women in Pennsylvania, "would benefit from more active voter participation and greater political representation in both the legislative and executive branches, since such voices could encourage more women-friendly policies enhancing their status in other areas."

In November of 1998, the Harrisburg Patriot-News concluded that "Pennsylvania voters elect fewer women to office than most states and women here have higher than average rates of death from breast and ovarian cancer." The Census Bureau reported that nationally the number of businesses owned by women in the United States reached 6.4 million in 1992, comprising 33 percent of all domestic firms. However, Pennsylvania ranks 49th in this category.

There also have been significant increases nationally in the number of women who go to college and those that major in traditionally-male degree program, such as engineering, business and management and biological and life sciences. Pennsylvania ranks 34th in this area, in the percentage of women with four or more years of college.

While women have made great strides economically and educationally, their number in the Pennsylvania House remains low. However small their number, they are considered a dedicated, intelligent group devoted to do the will of the people.

omen Members in House Leadership Positions

Caucus Leaders

The most senior woman in the House today is Representative Elinor Z. Taylor, who not only holds the record for the number of years served - - she began her 25th year in Harrisburg in 2001 - - but also serves as the Republican Caucus Secretary, a job she has held since 1995. Only two other women have served as caucus secretaries, Republican Marian Markley, of Lehigh County, who served from 1959 until 1966 and Democrat Marion L. Munley, of Lackawanna County, who served in the 1963-64 legislative session.

Only two other women have been elected to serve in caucus leadership positions. They are Mary Varallo, a Democrat from Philadelphia, who served as caucus chairman in the 1957-58 session and as majority whip in 1969 and Mae W. Kernaghan, a Republican from Delaware County, who served as caucus chairman from 1967 until 1970.

Women Speakers Pro Tempore

Representative Bentley, who served from 1923 until 1928, was a Republican from Crawford County and one of the first eight women elected to the House. She also was the first woman to serve as Speaker Pro Tempore and as a committee chair. Republican Representative Patricia Vance often is called upon today to serve as Speaker Pro Tempore by Speaker of the House Matthew J. Ryan.

51

Other Prominent Offices

Three women members have served in both the House and Senate of Pennsylvania. They are Democrat from Lehigh County, Jeanette F. Reibman, an attorney who retired from the Senate in 1994, and Democrat from Northampton County, Lisa M. Boscola who served in the House for four years beginning in 1995 and was elected to the Senate in November of 1998. Representative Shirley M. Kitchen, a Democrat from Philadelphia who served in the House in the 1987-88 session, was elected to the state Senate in 1996.

Others who left the House for Senate or cabinet-level offices include Representative Patricia A. Crawford, a Republican from Chester County, who served from 1969 until 1976, and was appointed Deputy Secretary of State in 1978 and served in that capacity until 1986. Democrat from Centre County, Helen Dickerson Wise, who served in the House during the 1977-78 session, was named Governor Robert P. Casey's Legislative Secretary early in his administration. She also served as a Casey senior advisor and as the liaison to his cabinet for several years.

Faith Ryan Whittlesey, a Republican from Delaware County who served from 1973-75, became the United States Ambassador to Switzerland.

Former state Senator Melissa Hart was elected to the U.S Congress in November of 2000, the first woman member of the state General Assembly to win a seat in the congress.

emographics

County Representation by Women

Thirty-two of Pennsylvania's 67 counties have sent women to Harrisburg.

Allegheny, Montgomery, Lehigh, and Philadelphia counties have had significant representation in the House by women compared to others.

Urban districts such as Allegheny County and Philadelphia County have elected a large percentage of the 105 women legislators.

Historically, these areas have been heavily Democratic, and women tend to have closer views to the liberal party. Districts in more conservative areas such as Lancaster County have had few women lawmakers. "Part of it has to do with the very conservative nature of the county," Amy Black, an assistant professor of government at Franklin and Marshall College, said, noting that, nationally, women tend to have views closer to Democrats than Republicans. "And within the Republican Party, the women who move up tend to be more moderate in their political views. Lancaster is very Republican and very conservative."

In the 1923-1924 session of the House six counties were represented: Allegheny, Butler, Cambria, Chester, Crawford and Philadelphia. Currently in the House, 28 women represent 32 counties. A complete list of the women by county can be found in the Appendices.

53

Party Affiliations of Women in the House

All of the women but one were either Republican or Democrat. A member of the Socialist Party once served in the General Assembly. There have been 64 Republican women and 40 Democrats. In 1993, one woman made a party switch from Democrat to Republican.

Lilith Martin Wilson, of Berks County was the General Assembly's only Socialist member. Elected in 1930, she also was the first Socialist woman to be named to any legislative body in the United States and the first woman candidate for governor of the Commonwealth. Her complete biography can be found in the "Biographies" section of this book.

Representative Patricia Carone Krebs was elected to the House in 1990 as a Democrat. She changed her party affiliation on December 7, 1993, joining the Republicans.

The only woman in the history of the House to switch parties, Carone attributed her switch to difficulties she was having with her Democrat leaders.

At the beginning of the 2001-2002 session there are 16 Republican women and 12 Democrat women.

Occupations Prior to House Service

The women who have served in the House have brought a tremendous amount of diversity to the institution. From housewife to psychologist, farmer to beautician, women legislators have come to Harrisburg trained in a broad range of occupations.

Although there is not one occupation among the women that

appears to be a stepping stone for election to the House, there are a few that some of the women share. Many early women listed their occupations as housewives. There are and were several attorneys, teachers and nurses.

Whatever the career path a woman followed before entering the House, that experience was also brought with her. For example, prior to her 1992 election, former Representative Katie True was a substance abuse writer and a tutor. Appropriately, she served as the chairman of the Health and Human Services Subcommittee on Drugs and Alcohol. In addition, she was the prime sponsor of the ZeroTolerance for underage drinking legislation.

A list of the women's occupations are included in this book's Appendices.

Average Age of Women When First Elected to the House

Women of all ages have served in the House. Most women, like their male colleagues, sought elected office during their middle-age years, between 45 and 54.

Some women lawmakers believe that married women do not come to Harrisburg earlier in their lives because of their family responsibilities as wives and mothers. Former Representative R.Tracy Seyfert, who turned 55 years old a month after her election and who holds a doctorate in psychology, said women begin their political careers later due to family responsibilities.

The youngest woman ever elected to the House was Frances Weston. Referred to as a "real ball of dynamite" by one GOP leader, she was only 26 years old when elected in 1980.

Representative Susie Monroe was the oldest woman ever elected to the House. Elected in 1948, she was 69 years old. She also was the first woman to die in office. After serving 20 years in the House, she was 89 years old when she died.

The youngest woman currently serving in the House is Representative Jennifer Mann. She is 30 years old. The oldest woman in the House, and longest serving, is Elinor Taylor, who is 79 years old.

Marital Status of Women in the House

It is important to examine the marital status of a woman who holds a political office. The marital status of a female legislator may also be related to her age at the time of her election to office. A younger woman may run while she is still single, whereas a married woman may wait to seek office until her children have grown.

The majority, or 65.35 percent, of the women who have served in the House were or are married.

Some women were married during their term in office. In fact, Representative Patricia Carone married Representative Edward Krebs on November 1, 1996, while both were members of the House.

Mothers in the House

It is sometimes difficult to fathom that a "driven" legislator fulfills any role besides that of a state representative. However, this role has taken "a back seat" to another, more important role for many House women - - motherhood.

Of the 105 women who have served in the House, 68 percent had children. The percentage of women in the House who were married is remarkably close to the percentage of women with children.

Whether or not a woman has children at home is significant. Many women in the General Assembly waited until their children were grown to pursue a career in politics. Representative Seyfert made the decision to wait until her children were grown. Representative Major, although she is not a mother, believes the most difficult challenge facing women candidates seeking public office is if she is raising children and maintaining a family life at the same time.

Representative Miller, whose daughter was seven years old during her first campaign for a House seat, only decided to run for office following a decision made by the entire family because everyone would be personally impacted by her choice.

Often, the experience women gain by raising families can be as valuable in the political arena as any professional experience.

Representative True has no regrets waiting until her sons were grown to pursue public office. She believes that her personal experiences with her family have made her more sympathetic to her constituents.

Women in the House Whose Husbands Also Served in the House

Twelve women had husbands who also served in the House. Most replaced their husbands following their deaths while in office.

Whether it be a special election, a general election or, in one extraordinary case, as a write-in candidate, the women who replaced their husbands did so with pride and determination. Laughlin replaced her husband, Representative Charles P. Laughlin, who served from 1973 until his death on April 10, 1988. She was elected in the general election the following fall as a write-in candidate.

Laughlin said that it was her terminally ill husband's wish that she run for his seat to ensure that his constituents would continue to receive the same level of service that he provided.

In an entirely different circumstance than that of the Laughlins, McHale replaced her husband Representative Paul McHale, who served from 1983-1991, in a special election on May 21, 1991 following his election to the U. S. Congress.

A complete list of the women whose husbands also served and other special elections of women in the House can be found in the Appendices.

iographies

Current Members

Baker, Jane S. (R) Lehigh County
Year of first legislative session – 2001

Baker was elected to the House following 15 years in local government as a Lehigh County commissioner and county executive. "Unlike many women running for the first time, I was fortunate," Baker said, "to not only have served in local government, but with an excellent track record."

The lawmaker served as county commissioner from 1986 until 1993. During that time she was elected vice chairwoman and then chairwoman of the commissioners. She served on the Judicial and Corrections committees and the Lehigh Parks Committee. In 1993 and again in 1997 Baker was elected county executive.

Like many female House members, Baker believes that fundraising is the most difficult challenge facing women candidates. In advising other women who might seek office, Baker recommends that they "participate in other campaigns to understand how they work... and don't be afraid."

Baker has a son and two daughters and has encouraged all of them to run for office. "Politics," she said, "always has been a part of their lives and each of them has the opportunity to serve the community."

When asked if she feels a bond with female legislators, Baker said, "my goal is to form a bond with all the legislators, men and women. I believe that should be the goal for all legislators."

Baker names two women as the most admired in Pennsylvania, First Lady Michele Ridge, for her outstanding contributions as the state's first lady, and Barbara Hafer because of her three successful runs for statewide office.

Baker's mother, a widow who raised three children who also was a leader in the community, including serving as president of the American Association of University Women, is one of her role models. Another is Judge Madaline Palladino.

Economic development, senior citizens and roads are priority issues with Baker, who "enjoys being able to communicate and work on the issues and concerns of those in the 134th district."

When asked to name those who helped her most in her political career, Baker said it would be difficult for her to single out any one individual. "I would say my family, my friends, my colleagues and the entire community," she said.

Since her election in November of 2000, Baker believes she has become more knowledgeable and aware of the needs of all the people in her district, including senior citizens, veterans, farmers, educators, and others.

For the 2001-2002 legislative session, Baker serves on the following committees: Health and Human Services, Intergovernmental Affairs, Labor Relations and Local Government.

Following her tenure in the House, Baker hopes to be remembered as "being available to all constituents and being their voice in Harrisburg by working on their issues and concerns at the state level."

"I would also like to be remembered for influencing other women to seek public office, " Baker said.

Bard, Ellen M. (R) Montgomery County
Year of first legislative session - 1995

Born January 11, 1949 in Minneapolis, Minn., the daughter of James D. and Elaine E. Bard, Representative Bard is married to Robert G. Stiratelli, Sc.D. and they have a daughter, Allison. Bard was raised in Anchorage, Alaska, and earned a bachelor of arts degree from Pamona College in Claremont, Calif., a Master of Science in Communication Research from Boston University in 1972, and a Master of Science in Management from the Sloan School, Massachusetts Institute of Technology (MIT), in 1980. A former business owner (TechLink Corp.), Bard has experience in the fields of synthetic fuels, banking and criminal justice.

Before running for statewide office, Bard served for four years as an Abington Township Commissioner. In her first election to the House - a four way race - she won with 55 percent of the vote. All of her opponents in both the primary and general elections have been men, and in her first election for state representative, an opponent berated her use of her maiden name, saying she "wasn't really married."

As a freshman legislator, Bard once was selected by Speaker Matthew J. Ryan to preside over the House.

Bard authored several important resolutions, budget amendments and numerous bills, many of which were signed into law, including: Act 19 of 1998, the Tax Collector Reform and Standardization law, providing oversight, standardized reporting procedures and timeframes for the state's elected local tax collectors; Act 198 of 1996, which stiffened penalties for graffiti crime; Act 75 of 1995, which authorized a special license plate to fund the Drug Abuse Resistance Education program in Pennsylvania schools; Act 65 of 1997, prohibiting unauthorized administration of date-rape drugs and providing additional penalties for drug-induced rape; and, Act 132 of 2000, providing for interest on overdue death benefits paid by insurance companies.

Bard's resolution regarding Holocaust education, preparedness for terroristic activities and energy as a national security issue led to significant reforms. She is standard-bearer for senior citizen tax relief, leading the legislature to expand the Property Tax/Rent Rebate Program in 1999. During the 2000 budget cycle, Bard successfully spearheaded implementation of per-pupil education budgeting.

Bard's recent legislative achievements include the passage of the following laws: Act 33 of 2000, which amends the law known as the Third Class City Code by providing for annual budgets, for uniform forms and for annual reports; Act 38 of 2000, which amends the law known as the First Class Township codes, by providing for school crossing guards, budget forms, filing copies and for uniform forms; and, Act 132 of 2000, which amends the law known as the Insurance Company Law of 1921, which changes requirements for the payment of life insurance benefits, allows the publication of rate increases on computer home pages and provides for coverage requirements for insulin and other blood sugar controlling agents; includes health maintenance organizations (HMOs) in conversion notifications; defines "long-term care" insurance, among other provisions.

Bard founded the environmental organization, *Earthright,* prior to holding elective office. More recently, she founded the local Citizens Trail Advisory Committee and continued to serve as a board member for several environmental organizations. Bard also serves on the advisory boards of Manor College and Penn State Abington College.

Bard's awards include the Griscom Award from Briar Bush Nature Center, "Legislator of the Year" from the Pennsylvania Tax Collector's Association, the "Community Service" award from Willow Grove Rotary, "Friend of Education" from the Abington School District, as well as recognition by the Holocaust Education Task Force.

When asked if she would encourage her daughter to run for public office, Bard replied that she had "mixed feelings . . . although elected office offers tremendous opportunities for public service, it can be a tough, demanding business with excessive time commitments and loss of family and private life."

Bard believes that female legislators are treated differently than males in the House. She cites not having enough information for decision-making because the informal communication channels - bars, golf games, dinners with lobbyists - don't include women, for the most part.

When asked if she is conscious that women are in the minority in the House, Bard replied "Absolutely. The lack of women in the House with seniority exacerbates the minority status. On the other hand, some extra opportunities are available… as a result of needing a female presence on committees. However, overall, females are not powerful."

Bard cited Paul Aloe, a retired Montgomery County political leader, Sunny Friedman, a committeewomen and former state legislative aide and Joanne Ayer, a committeewomen who helped her with fund raising, as three individuals who helped her the most in her public career.

For the 2001-2002 legislative session, Bard serves as the chairman of the House Subcommittee on Recreation. She also serves on the following committees: Local Government, Tourism and Recreational Development, Transportation and Urban Affairs.

Bard would like to be remembered as "someone who worked to make changes for the future, for the public good."

Bebko-Jones, Linda (D) Erie County
Year of first legislative session - 1993

Calling her father her role model who "suffered so many misfortunes in his life but continued to go on after every tragedy," Bebko-Jones said her father "taught her to be compassionate and caring of others. He gave me wings and told me I could be anything I wanted to be. He always supported me in all my endeavors."

The daughter of John and Joann Bebko, Bebko-Jones was born on May 1, 1946, in Erie. Married to the late Thomas Jones and the mother of two grown children, Bebko-Jones graduated from Villa Maria Academy for Girls in 1964 and attended Erie Business School. She has worked as a caseworker.

Bebko-Jones grew up in a "very political" family which exposed her to politics at an early age. Following a career working for both U. S. Senator Harris Wofford and state Senator Buzz Andrezeski, Bebko-Jones won her first election in 1992 by 74 votes after losing as a candidate in 1990. This first win captured an open seat in a race where she was the only woman running against five male candidates. In her second race, she ran against a male opponent as well.

When asked if members of the news-media treat female legislators differently than male legislators, Bebko-Jones wrote, "Yes. It seems they come to us only on social issues and not economic issues . . . if we are dealing with tax reform, they talk to my male counterparts. If we are dealing with AIDS, child care, they talk to me."

Health care, child care, and jobs are Bebko-Jones' major issues, and she is the prime sponsor of several measures, including bills in the areas of managed care, termination of parental rights, elections, insurance fraud, genetic testing and long term care for the elderly. She also has been active with sponsoring legislation concerning corrections employees, off-label drugs, jobs, tobacco settlement, adoption, and lighthouse licenses.

She feels her greatest accomplishment is having been "one of the prime sponsors of the stalking legislation, and seeing it passed, and raising awareness to addictions."

Bebko-Jones has been aggressive in promoting women in the legislature and for leadership posts. In 1997, she was unsuccessful in her bid for secretary of her caucus but she believed it was important for a woman to run since no woman was in Democratic leadership at that time. She said, "I do not believe we have all the faces of Pennsylvania in our leadership." She continued, "we're not out to use the power of the Legislature for ourselves, but rather to use that power to a positive end. Women have to work harder for acceptance and . . . do more homework than their male counterparts."

"It seems to me, that at the end of a long day on the House floor, the men all leave the Chamber carrying nothing and head-ing to Scott's (a popular bar near the Capitol), meanwhile, the women are lugging tons of paper back to their rooms to prepare for the next day,"

Bebko-Jones enjoys bringing her Erie constituents to Harrisburg to view the legislature at work in the historic House Chamber. "Quite frankly," she writes, "I am still in awe when I sit in my seat and look at William Penn."

For the 2001-2002 legislative session, Bebko-Jones serves as the chair of the Subcommittee on Drugs and Alcohol. She also serves on the following committees: Health and Human Services, Insurance and Veterans Affairs and Emergency Preparedness.

She would like to be remembered as someone who "was fair and wanted to change the quality of life not just for a certain class of people, but for all Pennsylvanians."

Bebko-Jones is a member of the Pennsylvania Commission For Women, numerous trustee and advisory boards and is the recipient of several state and local awards.

Bishop, Louise Williams (D) Philadelphia County
Year of first legislative session - 1989

An ordained Baptist Evangelical Minister and radio personality, Bishop was born on June 27, 1933, in Cairo, Georgia, the daughter of Sarah M. Hampton and Elijah Williams. She is the divorced mother of four children.

Bishop graduated from West Philadelphia High School in 1953 and the American Foundation of Dramatic Arts in 1955 with a degree in communications/radio broadcasting. She received an honorary degree from LaSalle University.

Bishop is a member of the National Political Congress of Black Women and the Pennsylvania Legislative Black Caucus, where she serves as co-chair. She is a member of the NAACP and the National Association of Women Clergy.

In 1992, Bishop attended the National Order of Women Legislators annual meeting, which met in Puerto Rico.

The recipient of several citations and awards, including "Woman Preacher of the Year," and woman and mother of the year awards, Bishop hosts "The Louise Williams Show" radio gospel program in Philadelphia on WDAS-AM.

In the 2001-2002 session, Bishop was chosen to serve as a member of the House Health and Human Services Committee and the chairman of its Subcommittee on Human Services, and also as a member of the Aging and Older Adult Services and State Government committees.

Cohen, Lita Indzel (R) Montgomery
Year of first legislative session - 1993

A business executive and attorney born in Philadelphia on December 20, 1940, the daughter of Joseph and Frances Banks Indzel, Cohen has two grown children and is a grandmother. Her husband, Stanley S. Cohen, also is an attorney. She recently listed him as the individual who helped her most in her public career.[184]

A 1962 cum laude graduate of the University of Pennsylvania, Cohen graduated from Penn's law school in 1965. She is a member of the Philadelphia, Montgomery County and Pennsylvania Supreme and Superior courts, the Montgomery County Bar Association, and served as assistant counsel for the Department of Housing and Urban Development and the Philadelphia School District.

She was the first woman ever appointed to any Lower Merion Township Commission, serving on the township Planning Commission from 1973 until 1985. From 1985 until 1993 Cohen served as township commissioner.

Considered by local government officials to be the "mother" of the City Avenue Special Services District, Cohen spearheaded the successful effort to improve City Avenue, or Route 1, the main traffic artery known as the "Golden Mile." Through her efforts, the first and only special services district in the nation was created with a partnership of two municipalities, Lower Merion Township and the City of Philadelphia.

The lawmaker was president of Lita Cohen Radio Services, Inc. from 1987 until 1994 and held a similar position with Orange Productions, Inc, a national radio syndication company, from 1983-1987. Prior to that she was executive vice president, general counsel and chief operating officer for the Independence and Banks Broadcasting Companies of Philadelphia, owners and operators of radio stations WHAT and WWDB. She got her start in business as president of "Gem Stones," a wholesaler of gems and minerals.

Cohen donates ten percent of her personal salary back to the community through COHEN C.A.R.E. (Community Advisory Reinvestment Effort). Instituted in 1992, this project has helped build a roller hockey rink for kids, purchase new playground equipment, plant trees, repair pedestrian walkways, placed a bench at a Veteran's War Memorial and purchase a portable public address system for police and civic groups.

Elected five times to the House, Cohen's first three opponents were male. She won her first election in 1992 with 70 percent of the vote.

Republican Cohen believes that former Democrat House Member and retired state Senator Jeanette Reibman is the most admired woman in Pennsylvania because of her "guts and intelligence." Her role model is federal judge Norma Shapiro."

House Resolutions designating April as Autism Awareness Month and March as Mental Retardation Awareness Month were both introduced by Cohen.

In 1994, she authored a major Lower Merion Township, Montgomery County, land bill. The measure authorized the township to sell and convey certain "Project 70" land free of restrictions imposed by a 1964 law.

In 1996, Cohen introduced legislation permitting non-profit cultural and state-chartered art museums to obtain temporary

67

liquor licenses and worked with the Senate to pass the Controlled Substance, Drug, Device and Cosmetic Act.

LAW In 1998, she amended the Administrative Code of 1929 to create the Osteoporosis Prevention and Education Program within the state Department of Health. She also prime a measure to provide for the *continuity of contract* under the monetary union in member states of the European Union. The latter provides that the new single currency "euro" shall be a commercially reasonable substitute and substantial equivalent to the ECU or European Currency Unit in contracts.

In the 1999-2000 Legislative Session, Cohen sponsored several bills, including measures preventing firearm trafficking, restricting gun possession privileges for certain offenses, and, strict laws punishing those who intimidate witnesses and victims, and for jury tampering. She also was the prime sponsor of the Prescription Contraception Equity Act, two hate crime bills, exemptions from realty transfer taxes and elimination of inheritance tax legislation.

In October of 2000, Cohen was named to co-chair the Majority Leader's Task Force on Child Care by House Majority Leader John M. Perzel. The task force finds ways for the legislature to help working families find safe, quality, affordable child care. Earlier in the year she mounted a cell phone collection to help victims of domestic violence, collecting hundreds of donated used cell phones to distribute to victims of abuse who can touch a pre-programmed button that automatically calls 911 for help in emergencies.

In addition to several other laws, Cohen was the prime sponsor of ACT 98 of 2000, the law that increases penalties for those who commit sex offenses against children by mandating counseling for prisoners while incarcerated.

Among honors Cohen has received are inclusion of Who's Who in American Women, as well as receiving the Humanitarian of the year Award from the Montgomery County Association of Retarded Persons and the "Legislator of the Year" award from the Pennsylvania chapter of the American Jewish Congress and NARAL-PA.

She was named "Woman of the Year" by the Conshohocken Business & Professional Women and the "Montgomery County Woman of Achievement Award" from the Montgomery County Chapter of the March of Dimes. Cohen also recently received the Philadelphia Region Hadassah "Person of the Year" award, the 2000 Philadelphia Business Journal Woman of Distinction Award for Public Service, and the 2001 Legislator of the Month by the National Association of Social Workers.

For the 2001-2002 legislative session, Cohen serves on the Judiciary Committee as the chairman of its Subcommittee on Crimes and Corrections, and also on the Appropriations, Children and Youth and Urban Affairs committees.

Dailey, Mary Ann R. (D'Altorio) (R)
Montgomery County
Year of first legislative session - 1999

Registered nurse and mother of three children, Dailey is the daughter of the late Henry and Viola Gentilo D'Altorio and is married to Jacob Dailey. In the primary election, Dailey ran against the party-endorsed candidate and two others. She won the primary by only 4 votes and went on to win the general election by 2,012 votes.

Dailey graduated from Presbyterian University Hospital School of Nursing and earned a bachelor's degree from Regents College and masters and doctoral (MSN and DNSC) degrees from Widener University.

The most difficult challenge facing women candidates, Dailey believes, is trying to balance the roles of wife, mother and politician, even with the wholehearted support of her family. She writes "I would advise women who are thinking of running for public office to realize the time commitment involved in public service.

This is not a job I would have considered while raising my children, for I believe that my responsibility to my family is my first concern. Now that they are grown, I can devote more time to full-time employment outside the home."

Dailey lists Dr. Clair Fagin, the former acting president of the University of Pennsylvania and the Dean of the university's School of Nursing as an outstanding, admirable professional, and her late aunt, Evelyn Gentilo Roscher as her role model. "Her untimely death at age 40 touched an entire community, for she was the victim of a head-on motor vehicle collision with a drunk driver," Daily wrote.

"The outpouring of community love that was witnessed at her funeral was a testament to her outstanding ability as a nurse... she had touched the lives of many … and countless numbers attended her funeral.

"It was for this reason that as a 12 year old child, I decided to carry on the tradition that Evelyn had started in her ministry of the sick and her advocacy on their behalf," Dailey said.

As a legislator Daily plans to introduce legislation that addresses the problem of "downskilling" of hospital staff and its effect on quality of patient care. In addition, she plans to work to limit taxes on individuals and business, to promote economic development in the state, and to improve police protection, especially in those neighborhoods where crime is rampant.

When asked who helped her the most in her political career, Dailey credits her husband, Jake, her manager Mike Pincus, her campaign committee chairman Don Bleim and her campaign treasurer, Tony Brasacchio.

Following her tenure in the House, Dailey would like to be remembered as someone who was responsible for a heightened awareness of healthcare issues and an improvement in the quality of patient care throughout the Commonwealth.

For the 2001-2002 session, Dailey, who serves on the Health and Human Services Committee, was named chairman of its Subcommittee on Health. She also serves on the Aging and

Older Adult Services, Intergovernmental Affairs and Professional Licensure committees.

Forcier, Teresa E. Brown (Fosberg) (R)
Crawford County
Year of first legislative session - 1991

The daughter of Waid "Fuz" and Elaine Augusta Swift Fosburg, Forcier was born on October 6, 1953, in Meadville. She graduated from Cambridge Springs High School in 1971 and attended both Alliance College and Edinboro University of Pennsylvania.

The mother of two grown children, and stepmother of two boys, Forcier believes that her parents were her role models. "I have always respected my parents and have learned a lot from both of them," she wrote.

In 1990, Forcier was encouraged to run for a seat in the House by key Republicans in Crawford County, the House Republican Campaign Committee and the Republican State Committee, Forcier defeated — by only 42 votes — Representative Connie Maine, a two-term incumbent.

"It was said," Forcier noted, "it would take a woman to defeat a woman."

As a legislator, Forcier's major issues include: supporting property rights, gun rights, right to life, sportsmen and women, emergency providers, rural issues and business issues. She considers her greatest accomplishment as an elected official as "being known in my district for working hard, and actually representing their views and opinions in Harrisburg."

Legislation sponsored by Forcier includes the Motorcycle Helmet Law. Forcier also introduced a resolution to designate the month of May as Motorcycle Safety Awareness Month in Pennsylvania. In addition, she introduces annually a resolution designating a week in May as "EMS Week."

In the 2001-2002 session, Forcier continues to serve as the

71

vice chair of the male-dominated Game and Fisheries Committee and on the Appropriations, Transportation and Veterans Affairs and Emergency Preparedness committees in the House. She lists her hobbies as motorcycling, hunting, fishing, trapping, and anything outdoors. She said she's "been fortunate to blend my pursuits with what issues I take up in the Legislature."

"When constituents want me to vote yes or no, I listen and vote accordingly. I am available and accessible and I don't skirt the issues," Forcier said.

Her most rewarding moment in the state legislature, Forcier wrote, is "Every time I am sworn in I am very proud and honored to be able to represent the people from the 6th legislative district for another term. Passing the modification of the motorcycle helmet law and having it signed into law will be a great accomplishment." The House passed her bill in late 2000, but the Senate did not have time to take action before adjournment.

Since her election, Forcier says she has changed. "I've grown in so many ways," she wrote. "I have become more vocal, positive, independent, and have tried to improve myself when it comes to speaking in public. I have learned to hold my own, worry about my district, and how to manage my time between political, legislative and personal commitments."

Harhart, Julie (Cihylik) (R)
Northampton, Lehigh Counties
Year of first legislative session - 1995

A lifelong resident of North Catasauqua and former legislative aide, Harhart graduated from Allentown Central High School in 1963 and Bethlehem Business School in 1965. She and her husband, Frank, are the parents of a married daughter.

Born August 7, 1945, to Frank and Theresa Cihylik, Harhart won her first election against an eight-year incumbent by only 63 votes. In all her elections since, her opponents have been male.

Harhart was the tax collector for the Borough of North Catasauqua from 1980 until 1988, and from 1990 to 1994 Harhart served as an office manager and as constituent liaison for a former state representative, working closely with Harrisburg and district office staffs.

Active in various community and church projects, Harhart also stays in touch with her constituents through her memberships in the Greater Northern Lehigh Chamber of Commerce, the United Northampton County Council of Republican Women, and the Lehigh County Council of Republican Women.

The recipient of several local and state awards, Harhart twice has been cited as a "Taxpayer Hero" from Citizens Against Higher Taxes, first in 1997 and again in 1998.

Among her other important measures, Harhart has introduced legislation to reduce government spending and waste, provide child-care tax credits, reduce tax liability for low-income families and create a new high technology alliance supporting university-based engineering research centers at Lehigh University and Carnegie Mellon University. She also has asked, through legislation, for a performance audit of the Commonwealth's children and youth agencies and has promoted safer schools by introducing a package of school violence prevention bills.

Harhart supported House Bill No. 1 in the 199-2000 session, which passed by a vote of 200-1. The measure raises the nontaxable income threshold for the poor.

In the 2001-2002 legislative session, Harhart serves as the vice chairman of the Children and Youth Committee. She also serves on the Health and Human Services, Intergovernmental Affairs and Professional Licensure committees.

Citing her father as her role model, Harhart wrote, "he was a solid family man, with a strong work ethic who never asked for anything... he was a quiet, understanding individual."

As a legislator, Harhart's major issues include property tax relief for low-income seniors, adoption, to help provide jobs in Pennsylvania, to help to re-train workforces in transition and to provide safe and secure schools. She feels her greatest accomplishment as a lawmaker was her statewide Safe and Secure School initiative, which was geared toward ending school violence.

Harper, Catherine "Kate" (R) Montgomery County
Year of first legislative session – 2001

Mother of two and lawmaker, Harper also is one of only a handful of Montgomery County lawyers to have argued a case before the United States Supreme Court.

Harper is the daughter of Thomas B. and Frances McCarron Harper who earned an undergraduate degree from LaSalle University and a law degree from Villanova University School of Law.

Prior to her 2000 election to the House, Harper was a community activist and a local and county government official for more than a dozen years. In 1986 she was appointed to the Lower Gwynedd Township Planning Commission and elected to her first term as township supervisor. She served as the chairman of the township board of supervisors for several years and is a past president of the Montgomery County Township Officials Association. Harper served on the county planning commission for six years and is a past vice chairman. She also is a past chairman of the county Open Space Planning Board and helped write the *Open Space Plan.*

A lawyer with a Fort Washington firm, Harper represents individuals, families, entrepreneurs and municipal agencies. She is a past director of the Montgomery Bar Association and past chairman of the organization's Judiciary and Long-Range Planning committees. She frequently lectures for township officials and lawyers on litigation and municipal law topics.

When asked about obstacles she faced when running for the House, Harper said she believes that most people in the district, "voters, party people and folks most likely to contribute to political causes, were simply used to men running. I felt I had to repeatedly validate myself as a serious candidate who had the skills, temperament and commitment both to win a hotly contested election, and then to serve as a member of the General Assembly."

"Fortunately," Harper continues, "having a background in both local government and as a local lawyer helped me with these things. Many people worried about how I was going to handle the campaign, the job of state representative 100 miles from home and my family."

When asked about those who supported her during the campaign, Harper was quick to point out that her husband, Paul J. Kelly, CPA, "rose to the challenge of helping me campaign, and keeping the home fires burning while I was out shaking hands. He also was a great emotional support when the negative campaigning started in earnest…"

Harper's great grandfather, Thomas B. Harper, was elected to the state Senate. Harper said he "promptly had a heart attack during his first term. Since he left a widow and nine children behind, that experience sort of soured the family on politics for a while."

Harper favors her aunt, Rosemary Flannery, as a role model. Flannery, Harper said, "became a lawyer with children at a time when there were very few women lawyers… she always has been supportive of me, and I do admire her."

The environment and dealing with urban sprawl, traffic, loss of open spaces and the like will be issues Harper will pay special attention to.

For the 2001-2002 legislative session, Harper serves on the Environmental Resources & Energy, Judiciary, Local Government and Transportation committees.

Harper hopes to "use the power and prestige of the office to help my community and the Commonwealth be a better place to live, work and raise a family. If I can do that, I will consider myself a success and worthy of the trust the voters have placed in me."

Josephs, Babette (D) Philadelphia County
Year of first legislative session - 1985

Attorney, author, and widowed mother of two, Josephs was born on August 4, 1949, in New York, the daughter of Eugene S. and Myra Josephs.

The widow of Herbert B. Newberg, Josephs is a 1962 graduate of Queens College, New York, and a 1976 graduate of Rutgers School of Law, in New Jersey.

Josephs is the author of two books — See How She Runs: A manual for committeepersons and Divorce Without a Lawyer. She is a member of the Pennsylvania American Civil Liberties Union and a co-founder and member of the National Abortion and Reproductive Rights Action League of Pennsylvania, and its foundation, the Clara Bell Duvall Education Fund. Josephs is a gay rights advocate.

A super delegate to the Democratic National Convention of 1992, she is a member of the following: five-county Democratic Women's Coalition, Philadelphia Bar Association, Liberty City Gay and Lesbian Democratic Club, Americans for Democratic Action and the American Jewish Congress.

The recipient of several awards, Josephs has been honored by the following: Citizen Action, Project Vote Smart, POPEC/ Triangle Interests, Public Interest Law Center of Philadelphia, National Abortion and Reproduction Rights Action League, and the Philadelphia Federation of Teachers, among others.

Josephs was named the chairman of the Subcommittee on Health and Human Services for the 2001-2002 legislative session. She also serves as a member of the Health and Human Services, Children and Youth, and Judiciary committees.

Laughlin, Susan (D) Beaver County
Year of first legislative session - 1989

Hoping to be remembered as a "true, honest and real servant of the people," Laughlin is the widow of Representative Charles P. Laughlin, who served in the House from 1973 until his death in 1988, the year Laughlin was elected in a write-in campaign.

"It was my terminally ill husband's wish that I run to fill his seat in the 16th district to ensure that constituents would continue to receive the same high level of service…" Laughlin recalled. Consequently, she organized a successful write-in campaign only 16 days prior to the election.

The daughter of Misag and Lucy Bogosian, Laughlin is the parent of two children - - a daughter, Sally, who is deceased, and a son, Thomas.

Laughlin believes that the most difficult challenges facing women candidates for public office are "being taken seriously, overcoming the 'old boys network,' and lack of clout."

She added that women thinking about running for political office should "be prepared… don't take opposition's remarks personally… treat constituents with genuine kindness and respect."

Ellen Casey, wife of former Governor Robert P. Casey, Laughlin believes, is the most admired woman in Pennsylvania, "for her strength and grace during her husband's illness." It is hard enough, Laughlin said, to go through something like that, and "even harder when you are in the public spotlight."

Legislation she is proud to have sponsored includes a bill that kept the homes of some of her constituents from being sold on the auction block and the institution of Aliquippa's two-tier tax system. Issues of major interest to Laughlin include education, "*real* tax reform," child care and senior citizen issues.

Laughlin is most proud of the service she provides to her constituents through obtaining state funds for a new road and overhead bridge in her district, securing the appropriation to support the historic site, Old Economy, and promoting tourism.

She has little appreciation of bureaucratic red tape and the slow process of law- making. Her most rewarding event in the House was the day she took the oath of office. "It was an honor to be sworn in to fill my husband's seat," Laughlin recalls.

For the 2001-2002 legislative session, Laughlin serves on the Consumer Affairs, Professional Licensure and Transportation committees.

Lederer, Marie A. (D) Philadelphia
Year of first legislative session - 1993

The daughter of Donato and Edith Panosetti Lederer, the lawmaker is married to Judge William J. Lederer, whom she credits with helping her most in her public career, and they have three children.

Motivated to run for the House as a mother and grandmother, Lederer is interested primarily in quality of life issues such as juvenile street crime, drugs, child care and assistance for senior citizens.

She is a former special assistant to Congressman Joseph F. Smith and has close ties with Temple University, where she attended college and taught political science courses.

In her first campaign for a House seat, she faced a candidate who was the editor of a local newspaper, which covered most of the district.

Lederer was a delegate to the Democratic National Conventions of 1976 and 1980 and served as the whip of the Philadelphia delegation. Also, she was the registration chair of Philadelphia County in 1984, a member of the Democratic State Committee from 1980 through 1994, and served as a committeewoman and officer of the Democratic Women of Philadelphia in the 1970s and 1980s.

Raising money, Lederer believes, is the most difficult challenge facing women candidates for public office.

She gave the following advice to women considering running for public office: "If you have minor children, it is not a good career. Children need their mothers on location."

Lederer's mother, whom she admires above all women in Pennsylvania, encouraged her to run for office and Lederer would encourage her own daughter to run, if that was her daughter's choice.

Lederer's pride in her mother's legacy is revealed in the following story: "Born on the 4th of July in 1907, my mother successfully organized the first three Ladies Knitgoods Union shops in Philadelphia and in Pennsylvania against the wishes of an all-male industry. Her ability to lobby for better pay and working conditions for her fellow workers taught me at a very young age to always look out for my colleagues as well."

While she believes that the news media treats women fairly, Lederer wrote that the women members of the House are treated differently by male legislators who feel naturally superior to all women. She also feels that she has found great cooperation "from my colleagues on both sides of the aisle," and she tries to return the same.

Her major issues in the House concern juvenile crime, transportation, elevating the quality of life for senior citizens and tourism. Creating jobs also is at the top of her list and during her tenure, Lederer was successful in convincing the second largest tuna packing plant in the world to open its U.S. subsidiary in her Philadelphia district rather than in San Diego, Calif.

She would improve the House by allowing representatives to hire more district office staff. "I disagree with my leadership who say the real work is done in Harrisburg. If my constituents are not serviced in my district on a daily basis, there never would be a Harrisburg staff."

For the 2001-2002 legislative session, Lederer was chosen to serve as the House Urban Affairs Committee's chairman of the Subcommittee on First Class Cities and Counties. She also is a member of the Agriculture and Rural Affairs and the Tourism and Recreational Development committees.

Lederer would like to be remembered as "that one politician who kept every campaign promise."

Mackereth, Beverly L. (R) York County
Year of first legislative session – 2001

Mayor of Spring Grove Township, mother of four, community activist and lawmaker, Mackereth came to the House following 20 years as a public servant in York County.

Mackereth is the former executive director of Healthy York County Coalition, deputy director of the Governor's Community Partnership, and former programs manager and director of the Child Abuse Unit of the York County District Attorney's Office. She serves on the advisory board of York County Children & Youth Services as well at Attoeney General Mike Fisher's Medical/Legal Advisory Board. She earned a Bachelor of Arts degree from Frostburg State University in Maryland.

Running for the House in 2000 with the full support of her family, Mackereth's female opponent in the primary tried to use the fact that she was the mother of four negatively. That is, that she should stay at home and take care of her family.

In offering advice to other women thinking of running for public office, Mackereth said, "Just make sure you have a strong support system before making the decision to run." She also would encourage her daughter to run for office, and would "be there to offer support and assistance."

As a legislator, Mackereth has chosen to focus on education – improving our public schools and funding – tax reform, healthcare – especially the costs of prescriptions, and transportation. She enjoys answering constituent questions and researching policy issues in her new position, and enjoys campaigning least.

When asked who helped her most in her public career Mackereth cited the following York County officials: Sheriff Bill

80

Hose, Register of Wills Brad Jacobs and District Attorney Stan Rebert. She also listed the members of the House York County Delegation, including Representatives Mike Waugh, Steve Nickol, Stan Saylor, Rom Miller and Bruce Smith.

Mackereth is a more confident person having run successfully for her seat and said her new job will help her "learn a great deal about a variety of issues."

She would like to be remembered as "an effective, honest, legislator who represented the people of the 196th district well."

Major, Sandra J. (R) Susquehanna County
Year of first legislative session - 1995

A woman who wishes to be remembered as "an individual who had genuine compassion for and sincere interest in" the people in her legislative district, Major won her election to the House by a 20 percent margin (approximately 60 percent vs. opponent's 40 percent).

Born in 1954, the daughter of H. William Major and Barbara Wescott Rydzewski, "Sandy" graduated from Keystone College and continued studying at the University of Scranton.

Motivated to run following her work as a legislative aide to the late Representative Carmel Sirianni, Major felt that being a "single woman" was a great obstacle in her political race.

As a political candidate she did not feel that her opponent publicly used her gender in a negative way, but "there was an undercurrent referring to my ability to do the job because I was a woman."

She does believe that it would be "challenging" to be a legislator and also a mother and wife attempting to raise children and maintain a home-life for family.

Major's grandfather is Representative Harold G. Wescott who served in the House from 1945 until 1962.

Prior to her service in the House, Major was the Susquehanna

81

County Treasurer from 1991 until 1995.

"Work hard," Major says to other women thinking of running for public office, and "you can achieve your goals."

If she had a daughter, Major would encourage her to run for public office because she feels that "women are wonderful detail people and make wonderful candidates for public office." She warns, however, that the "good old boys network" is still strong in Harrisburg. While the network is strong, Major believes the male members of the House are very polite to female members.[215]

Citing her mother as her role model, Major gives much credit to the success of her political campaigns to both her mother and her sister, Billie Kaye Kraus, a former House legislative aide who now serves as the Director of Government Relations for the state Department of Education.

According to Major, primary areas of concern for the lawmaker are local government, dairy and agricultural issues. One of the things she likes about being a legislator is rewarding people for their achievements, such as Eagle Scouts and talented artists and musicians.

"All the paperwork" is enjoyed least by Major. In order to improve the House of Representatives, which she believes "overall, works well," Major suggests the removal of the television cameras from the floor. Then the "grand standing" by some members will be cut back.

For the 2001-2002 legislative session, Major serves as the secretary of the House Ethics Committee. She also serves on the Agriculture and Rural Affairs, Game and Fisheries, Local Government and Professional Licensure Committees.

Manderino, Kathy M. (D) Philadelphia
Year of first legislative session - 1993

A lawyer who twice convinced insurance carriers to reverse decisions and agree to cover the cost of constituents' successful organ transplants, Manderino considers the ability to make a real difference in people's lives one of the greatest aspects of public service. The daughter of the late James J. Manderino, legendary and respected Speaker of the House, and Constance A. Myers Manderino, the lawmaker claims her parents as her role models.

Born in Monessen, Westmoreland County, where her father served as legislator, Manderino located across the state after graduating from Penn State with a degree in public service. She worked for nine years in economic development and labor-management relations and attained her law degree at night from Temple University. She was a litigation attorney for a major Philadelphia law firm before being elected to represent Philadelphia's 194th legislative district.

Because she was not a native of her district, she faced "carpetbagger" accusations in her first election when she beat two men in the primary and another in the general election. "I countered their criticism by pointing out that, I may not have been born in the district, but I made an affirmative choice as an adult to live here because it's a great community," Manderino said.

In addition to the "carpetbagger" reference in her first election, Manderino recalls one opponent during a public debate suggesting that a "married, family man can better represent the community than a single woman." Single or married, Manderino believes that often women are reluctant to put themselves forth as candidates. Also, in today's races women are usually challengers trying to overcome the power of the incumbent. Advice she would offer to other women thinking of running for political office includes: 1) just do it... 2) you have to be willing to ask your friends for money, and 3) it's well worth it.

Manderino believes that being an elected representative of the people is a high calling. If she had a daughter she would encourage her to run for public office. "I would want her to be a part of the process and give back to society in that way," she said. Still, Manderino believes that their colleagues treat female legislators somewhat differently than male legislators. "I think there still exists an informal 'boys club' of socializing and doing business at the same time, and that women often are not part of that club," she said.

Policymaking and politics are approached differently by women, Manderino noted, continuing, "I think our approach is equally valid and important, but because women are so much in the minority, there is a lack of balance of perspectives in the process."

Manderino has been the prime sponsor of several pieces of important legislation, including health care insurance market reform, nursing care quality indicators, daycare subsidy funding, and crime victims impact testimony. Her major issues of concern are health-care, economic and social justice, and economic development.

Manderino rates fundraising as her least favorite campaign job. She would improve the operations of the House by making the "internal workings a little less seniority driven. Diversity and inclusion often faced the biggest obstacles in 'the way it's always been done.'"

In listing those who have helped her most in her public career, Manderino lists Dick Hayden, her predecessor, for recruiting her, her committee people and volunteers for vesting confidence in her candidacy, and the voters for electing and returning her to office. Internally, she commends Democratic Appropriations Chairman Rep. Dwight Evans (D-Philadelphia) for promoting women in general and her in particular.

For the 2001-2002 legislative session, Manderino serves as the secretary of the Insurance Committee of the House. She also is a member of the Appropriations, Children and Youth and Judiciary committees.

As for what she hopes her legacy in the House will be, Manderino would like to be remembered this way: she cared, she acted, she made a difference.

Mann, Jennifer L. (D) Lehigh
Year of first legislative session - 1998

A Lehigh County single businesswoman who formerly owned Instant Access, a pager service company, Mann is a graduate of Lehigh University with a degree in economics and government. Born in 1969, Mann is the daughter of David R. and Gloria Loponzski Mann. She has served on the board of Junior Achievement of Lehigh Valley and is a member of the Allentown Business Council of the Lehigh Valley Chamber of Commerce. Mann also serves as a member of the Hamilton Park Crime Watch.

While in the House, she has served on the Environmental Resources and Energy, Finance, and Urban Affairs committees. Mann serves as the secretary of the Finance Committee for the 2001-2002 session.

Mann serves as co-chair of "The House the House Built," a Habitat for Humanity project. Led by Mann, members and staff of the state House will build a duplex in the city of Harrisburg for two local, low-income families.

Women legislators offer a "viewpoint that I believe is often missing from our representative government," Mann said.

Miller, Sheila M. (R) Berks
Year of first legislative session - 1993

A farmer, wife, mother, and science honors graduate of The Pennsylvania State University, Miller is the daughter of Vernon J. and Mildred A. Heberling Miller. The former director of the state Senate Agriculture and Rural Affairs Committee from 1983 through 1992, Miller ran for office following the retirement of veteran Representative John Davies.

Miller is proud of her political heritage — she is a distant relative of U.S. President Dwight D. Eisenhower.

Miller kept her job in the senate while running for election to the House. She skillfully and successfully combined farming, family, career and campaigning. She campaigned door-to-door during her "spare time."

In the 1992 primary, Miller ran against six men and defeated another woman in the general election. In 1994, she defeated a male opponent and a female opponent in 1996. She had no opposition in the 1998 election.

Lack of financial and traditional organizational support were cited as her greatest challenges as a woman candidate, but they were "not insurmountable."

"You must be committed to running and you must anticipate having to do most of the work yourself. You must be willing to have your life and family scrutinized and you must be willing to always give 150 percent because people will be expecting more from a women," the lawmaker advised.

When asked if she would encourage her daughter to run for office, Miller said that her daughter, Emilie, who now is 14 years old, was asked when she was 11 years old if she had future plans to run for political office. An Associated Press reporter wrote that Emilie said, "I see how hard my mom works and how long her days are, and I'd rather do something that doesn't take up so much time." In response, Miller told her not to close any doors because she doesn't know today what she may be asked to do tomorrow.

Miller believes that women are treated differently than men in the House. "But that does not mean that it is a negative situation. Generally, the language used around women members is appropriate and respectable. As women, we are different than our male counterparts; we work together and use our strengths in a field that is still predominantly male," she offered.

Nonetheless, "the women legislators are as different from one another as our male counterparts," Miller said, adding, "we {men and women} represent different parts of the Commonwealth and different philosophies. On the whole, however, I see that women legislators are thorough in their research and follow through and I appreciate and trust their opinions."

Citing fellow Representative Elinor Taylor (R-Chester County) as someone she admires, Miller says that Taylor is "respected for her determination and assertiveness as a legislator, as well as her concern for other women legislators."

Miller's father and sister are her role models. Her father served in the U.S. Marines during World War II and received a Purple Heart for injuries sustained at Iwo Jima. He also never hesitated to ask her to do jobs on the farm, showing her that any task can be accomplished if one works at it, whether "you are a boy or a girl." Miller's sister, a Ph.D., is the head of the biology department at Davidson College in North Carolina.

Miller hopes her efforts on behalf of the agriculture industry will keep "it a leader in our Commonwealth and in Berks County throughout the next century and for generations to come. No farmers, no food!" She hopes the services she provides to her constituents make beneficial changes in their lives.

For the 2001-2002 legislative session Miller serves on the following committees: Agriculture and Rural Affairs, Children and Youth, Game and Fisheries and Tourism and Recreational Development.

"If I can help to make our Commonwealth a stronger, safer state through the law making process, I will have succeeded in accomplishing my legislative goal," Miller concluded.

Mundy, Phyllis Block (D) Luzerne
Year of first legislative session - 1991

Mundy was born in 1948 in Evansville, Ind., the daughter of William and Barbara Aman Block. Mundy resides in Kingston and has a son and grandson.

In 1970, Mundy graduated from Bloomsburg University of Pennsylvania with a degree in secondary education and French. In 1995, she was recognized by her college's alumni association for distinguished service.

Prior to her service in the House, Mundy was business manager of a multi-million dollar manufacturing facility. Her volunteer work in the community includes work with the League of Women Voters, the Junior League, the Domestic Violence Service Center, Volunteers for Literacy, and the Big Brothers/Big Sisters program.

She was a member of the Luzerne County Board of Elections from 1987-88.

"I consistently fight for and promote legislation to improve access to affordable healthcare, to improve academic achievement in our public schools, and to enhance opportunities for good jobs with good wages and benefits for area residents," Mundy said.

"Whether working to assure that my district receives its fair share of state tax dollars for community projects, or influencing legislation which affects us daily, I strive to provide the necessary leadership while maintaining the highest personal and professional standards."

Mundy serves on the board of the Greater Pittston Chamber of Commerce, the advisory committee of the Domestic Violence Service Center and the board of Emergency Medical Services of Northeastern Pennsylvania.

The lawmaker is a member of Common Cause, the Sierra Club and is the past president of the League of Women Voters of the Wilkes-Barre area. Named as a Wyoming Valley Women's Network *Pathfinder,* she also was named "Legislator of the Year" by the Pennsylvania Mental Health Counselors Association.

In 1997, Mundy was honored as a "Guardian of Small Business" by the National Federation of Independent Businesses. More recently, Mundy received the Athena Award from the Greater Wilkes-Barre Chamber of Commerce, "Outstanding Elected Woman of the Year" award from the Pennsylvania Federation of Democratic Women, and the "John Heinz Friend of

Nursing Award."

In the House, for the 2001-2002 legislative session, Mundy serves as the chairman of the Subcommittee on Education. In addition, she serves on the Children and Youth, Commerce and Economic Development, and Education committees.

Orie, Jane Clare (R) Allegheny
Year of first legislative session - 1997

One of 15 politicians from across the country featured in a 2000 video documentary, "Women in Politics," attorney and legislator Orie has received national attention for a number of her initiatives and efforts while serving in House.

The documentary "spotlighted" a diverse group of women politicians who serve at the federal, state and local levels. Orie was chosen for her work on such issues as child abuse, domestic violence and school violence, as well as for her reputation as a role model for young women. Broadcast on *Lifetime,* the cable television channel for women, the documentary's producers hope to "educate and inspire young women, so that they will become involved in the political process."

Orie, a lifelong resident of McCandless Township, was born in 1961 in Pittsburgh, the daughter of Dr. John R. and Patricia R. Lally Orie. As a ten year veteran prosecutor, Orie worked as a deputy attorney general in the Division of Criminal Prosecution and as an assistant Allegheny County district attorney where she was elevated, due to her high conviction rate, to the divisions of Homicides and Crimes Against Persons. The lawmaker is a 1984 graduate of Franklin & Marshall College and a 1987 graduate of Duquesne Law School.

Since taking office in 1997, Orie has been the prime sponsor of over 125 pieces of legislation. Currently, Orie serves on the Appropriations, Judiciary, Health and Human Services, and the Republican Policy committees and chairs the Health and Human

Services Subcommittee on Drugs and Alcohol.

Orie has been instrumental in working to strengthen the state's domestic violence laws and fighting to provide victims with more rights. Orie's Domestic Violence Health Care Response Act, signed by Governor Tom Ridge in late 1998, made Pennsylvania the first state in the nation to institute universal screening and medical advocacy for victims of domestic violence. This legislation gave Pennsylvania the only "A" grade in domestic violence response as rated by the Family Violence Prevention Fund. As a result of this bill, Orie became the first Pennsylvania state legislator to be invited to speak at the National Conference on Health Care and Domestic Violence.

In addition, her work in strengthening Pennsylvania's *Megan's Law* and drunk driving laws has earned statewide and national attention.

In fact, Orie introduced the law that requires ignition interlock devices to be installed in cars of convicted drunk drivers. If the small, breath testing device detects even a quarter of the legal limit of alcohol on the driver's breath, the vehicle will not start.

She also introduced several amendments to legislation to help limit the impact of the recent Allegheny County property reassessment on low-income residents.

In a newspaper interview in the spring of 2000, Orie reported that being a woman hasn't held her back in the legislature. She credited her persistence, experience and dedication to public service as having contributed to her success… "I've been passing legislation, and I'm proud of what I've been able to accomplish in just two terms as a legislator" she was quoted.

To foster more interest in politics, Orie said in the same interview, that she talks to women at meetings and encourages college students to sign up for internships in her office.

"I always strongly encourage young women to pursue the path of public service because I think the political landscape as a whole needs more women to participate," Orie said, adding, "I believe the political arena would certainly benefit from their talents, compassion and commitment. Women can bring so much experience and insight to the table on issues."

Orie added, "Women are half of the population and we bring unique ideas, opinions and issues to the forefront. Without participation by women, we are only looking at problems and policies from a limited perspective."

Orie was honored with the 2000 Reader's Choice Award as the "Best Public Official" from Gateway Publications, an award voted on by her constituents.

For the 2001-2002 legislative session, Orie was named as the chairman of the House Subcommittee on Drugs and Alcohol. She also serves on the Appropriations and Judiciary committees.

Pickett, Tina L. (R) Bradford
Year of first legislative session – 2001

Bradford County commissioner, hotel owner, mother and now, lawmaker, Pickett won her first election to the House by earning 68 percent of the vote.

Pickett served as the president of the Wysox Municipal Sewer Authority and as vice president of Partners in Family and Community Development. She was the president of the Towanda Lions Club and past president of the Central Bradford Chamber of Commerce.[227]

Pickett, who has studied business, marketing and culinary arts, owns the Williamston Inn. She served two terms as a county commissioner, from 1996 until 2000, and is the first woman elected to represent the 110th legislative district.

When asked if her decision to run for public office was supported by her family, Pickett replied, "yes, although initially my mom, who is 80 years old, was concerned about a perceived lack of integrity in higher government."

Fundraising is considered by Pickett to be the most difficult challenge facing women candidates for public office. In advising other women who may think of running for public office, Pickett recommends that candidates "prepare with lots of community service and arrange your life to handle nights and weekends in the constituency."

Pickett would encourage her daughter, Lynne, to run for public office. "I would be delighted to assist in her campaign if she chose to run" Pickett said.

While relatively new in her position, Pickett believes that female legislators are treated differently than male legislators by other legislators. She said that the "male network is still a bit stronger." She said she is conscious that she is a minority in the House, but that "it is not a negative."

Michele Ridge and her "great family image," Pickett believes is the most admired woman in Pennsylvania. "She is respected as intelligent and involved with effective issues," Pickett said. Friend and mentor Betty Reuter is her role model. "She is gracious, intelligent, still is youthful yet in her 70s... is fun loving, successful, community oriented and a great hostess," said Pickett.

As a lawmaker, Pickett has chosen rural economy, preservation of rural life and values, senior women with low incomes, small businesses and downtowns as important issues.

Citing her January 2, 2001, swearing-in ceremony as a rewarding moment in her life, Pickett said that "touring my district and talking to constituents and finding solutions for their problems" is the aspect of her legislative work that she enjoys most.[230]

Pickett says she has changed since her election to the House. "I must be more focused due to {new} time constraints and be willing to delegate and empower my staff."

She would like to be remembered as an accessible, knowledgeable and inspiring lawmaker.

Rubley, Carole A. (R) Chester
Year of first legislative session - 1993

Hoping to be remembered as a caring legislator who brought

state government to the local people, Rubley, who has been interested in politics since high school, is the mother of three grown children. She is married to C. Ronald Rubley and was born in 1939, in Bethel, Conn., the daughter of George and Evelyn Maloney Drumm.

A graduate of Albertus Magnus College in Connecticut with a degree in biology, Rubley also earned a master's degree in environmental health from West Chester University of Pennsylvania. Rubley served as the Chester County Solid Waste Coordinator for six years. A former environmental consultant, Rubley has served as a member of several environmental organizations, often as a member of a board of directors.

In 1992, the year of her first House campaign, Rubley won with 58.5 percent of the vote.

Her prior elected positions include the Tredyffrin Township Board of Supervisors, where she served from 1988-92, and she spent 10 years as a member of the Tredyffrin Township Planning Commission and chaired the Chester County Eastern Regional Planning Commission.

Fundraising and "getting fair newspaper coverage," Rubley believes, are the most difficult challenges facing women candidates for public office.

Advice she would offer women who are thinking of running for public office includes, "develop a strong group of supporters. Be careful in the selection of a consultant… {one} needs to ensure that they will work with you on your issues and in a manner that is comfortable for you."

When asked if she thinks female legislators are treated differently than male legislators by colleagues, Rubley believes, "it is more difficult to be included. The males tend to gather in a manner and at functions that aren't easy for women to participate in. For example, bars, golf outings, cigar sessions."

Rubley has no gender preference in choosing legislative staff. While all the employees in Rubley's offices happen to be female, she has sponsored male interns.

Rubley's major issues are environmental and land use, local tax reform and business tax reduction. She has sponsored bills on local tax reform, pesticide notification, trademark registration, geologic survey and infant crib safety. Rubley represented the House on the Governor's 21st Century Environment Commission.

Rubley cites her campaign manager in early elections, Linda Peterson, as someone who has helped her most in her public career. Peterson was the one who actually "sought me out to run for office," Rubley said. She also gives credit to her office staff. They are "extremely helpful to me because of their great constituent work," she said.

The League of Women Voters of the Upper Main Line selected Rubley as its Involved Voter of the Year (IVY) in 1993 and she received the Woman of Achievement Award from the Chester County March of Dimes in 1997.

For the 2001-2002 legislative session, Rubley serves on the Children and Youth, Consumer Affairs, Environmental Resources and Finance committees. She chairs the Subcommittee on Parks and Forests.

Steelman, Ph.D., Sara Gerling (D) Indiana
Year of first legislative session - 1991

A graduate with a degree in zoology from the University of Chicago who also earned a Ph.D. in genetics from Stanford University, Steelman is a former educator and journalist.

Born in 1946, in Wichita, Kansas, the daughter of Paul H. and Amy G. Gerling, Steelman taught college psychobiology and psychology and was a freelance journalist and editor.

Active in the American Association of University Women, Steelman was a member, in many cases a board member or officer, of several statewide organizations. They include the Indiana County Historical & Genealogical Society, League of Women Voters, Rotary, Pennsylvania Association for Sustain-

94

able Agriculture, and Zonta. She also served as an advisory board member of the Mental Health Association of Indiana County, the Indiana Arts Council and was on the board of the Indiana Symphony.

In 1992, Steelman was named one of Indiana's American Association of University Women's "Notable Women" and received, the same year, the Keystone Press Award for investigative reporting. The next year she received the Chevy Chase Community Center's Humanitarian Award. In 1994 she was honored by the Alice Paul House Community Service Award for Service to Victims of Violence.

Married to John Henry Steelman, they have a daughter, Amy.

In the 2001-2002 legislative session, Steelman was named vice chairman of the Agriculture and Rural Affairs Committee. She also was named to the Education, Environmental Resurces & Energy and Finance committees.

Taylor, Elinor Gene Zimmerman (R) Chester
Year of first legislative session - 1977

First elected in November of 1976, Taylor is the longest serving woman in the history of the Pennsylvania House of Representatives. For the past 24 years, "EZ" Taylor has represented Chester County's 156th legislative district.

Considered by colleagues as the Republican Caucus's senior stateswoman and a true "team player," Taylor was elected Majority Caucus Secretary in 1995. She was reelected to that prestigious post in both 1997 and 1999. Currently, Taylor is the only woman in the state House and Senate with a caucus leadership position.

Taylor also serves as the chair of the board of directors of the Pennsylvania Higher Education Assistance Agency (PHEAA).

Born in 1921 in Norristown, she is the daughter of Harold I. and Ruth A. Rahn Zimmerman. Married to William M. Taylor,

95

they are the parents of a daughter, Barbara R. Taylor (Mrs. Gerald Zarella) and five grandchildren.

Taylor has a bachelor's degree from West Chester University of Pennsylvania and a master's degree in education from Temple University. She also has studied at the University of Delaware and Columbia University. Taylor taught at Ridley Park High School and West Chester State College (now University) and served for eight years as the college's Dean of Administration.

She holds the title of Professor Emeritus, West Chester University, and is the 1996 recipient of a Doctor of Public Service honoris causa from West Chester University of Pennsylvania.

Taylor served on the West Chester Borough Council from 1974-78 as the first women ever elected to that office. In 1976, Taylor reflected that "it was not popular for women to run for public office." In fact, the year she was elected, only three Republican women were elected to the House.

Taylor believes that one of the most difficult challenges facing women candidates for public office is gaining the respect of male colleagues. Women, she says, should "try not to be threatening to men. Most men who have confidence in themselves and who do not have fragile 'ego' can accept contributions and suggestions from women," Taylor said.

The advice she offers to other women who are thinking of running for office includes: "have a life before Harrisburg; be able to make decisions; bring to public office real life experience, not text book learning; and, see yourself as someone willing to serve – not 'what's in it for me.'"

Taylor, who feels a strong bond with other Republican women legislators, believes that anthropologist Margaret Mead (1901-1978) is the most admired woman in Pennsylvania. Her role models include Jeane J. Kirkpatrick and Barbara Bush.

As a legislator, Taylor's major issues include basic and higher education, including charter schools, schools of choice, student grants and loans, and the tuition account program, among others. She also has a deep interest in the health and welfare issues of long-term and "uncompensated" care for the elderly, and child care.

Taylor's honors include the Outstanding Alumni Award from the Alumni Association of West Chester State College, the Outstanding Citizens of 1984 Award from the Greater West Chester Chamber of Commerce, the George Washington Honor Medal from the Freedoms Foundation at Valley Forge, the Ben Franklin Medal for Distinguished Achievement in Higher Education, Order of the Owl, from Temple University, West Chester University Hall of Fame, and Chapel of the Four Chaplains Legion of Honor Award, among others.

She also is the recipient of the Senator John Heinz Memorial Award – National Adult Day Services Association 2000, The Immaculata Medal – Immaculata College.

Taylor cited the late Representative Carmel Sirianni and former state Senator Earl Baker as two individuals who helped her the most in her public career.

When asked how she has changed since her election, Taylor said that "coming {to the House} from 25 years in academia, I thought the issues would be addressed in a logical manner. I found out early on that every move would be looked upon politically as well as for its real worth. I learned the system - maybe that's not so good - it seems that the squeaky wheel gets the attention and the good guys are ignored."

Taylor is married to William M. Taylor.

In the 2001-2002 legislative session, Taylor is the only woman to serve on the 21-member Rules Committee.

She would like to be remembered as a leader "who was feisty but fair; as a compassionate representative who tackled the little things as well as those that might be considered big; and, as a woman who never asked for anything more than she needed but never gave anything less than her best effort."

Vance, Patricia Huston (R) Cumberland
Year of first legislative session - 1991

A registered nurse who often serves as Speaker Pro Tempore, Vance was born in 1936, in Williamsport, the daughter of Frederick B. and Mary Yontz Huston Vance. She is married to Charles D. Vance and they have two sons.

Prior to her House service, Vance served as the Cumberland County Recorder of Deeds from 1978-1990. She was the first woman elected to county office in Cumberland County. She is a graduate of the Harrisburg Hospital School of Nursing.

She was motivated to run for House election because she wanted "to have subjects viewed from a different perspective, and perhaps naively, to 'make a difference' in people's lives." In her first election she ran in a heated four-way primary. She was outspent by her opponents and had to overcome voters' fears that she might not be tough enough to stand up to the rough and tumble of the House.

As a candidate, one of her opponents used her gender in a negative way. The worst example was "a letter to the editor just before the primary, urging voters not to vote for me just because I was 'an accident of birth.'" She feels that her most difficult challenge as a lawmaker is raising money.

She would advise women who are thinking of running for office to "obtain an education and solid career before running for full-time public office. Develop expertise and confidence in your own abilities first. Perhaps run for local office first."

Ever the cheerleader of women in politics, in a fall, 1998 speech to members of the Pennsylvania Federation of Business and Professional Women's Clubs, Vance said, "I would implore you to care enough about the community where you live to become involved in a large way, or a small way. You have the intelligence and creativity – I ask you to use it to improve your community."

Vance believes that female legislators are treated differently than male legislators by their peers "to a small degree." She, however, finds greater discrimination in the general public and in the media. She said, "members of the media, perhaps inadvertently, usually refer to male legislators as Representative so and so, while she is almost always referred to in news stories as Mrs. Vance.

When asked about a role model, Vance said she has always admired Margaret Thatcher, especially for her outspoken courage.

Health care, long term care for the elderly and insurance are Vance's major issues. To that end, she was the prime sponsor of several major laws, including the following: Act 24 of 1996, a law prohibiting insurance discrimination of victims of domestic violence; Act 13 of 1997, and elder abuse prevention and reporting law; Act 53 of 1997, which requires more parental input in children's drug and alcohol problems; and, Act 68 of 1998, managed care legislation.

Also, in September of 2000, she proposed the Pennsylvania Extraordinary Prescription Plan, legislation providing citizens age 19 and older eligibility in a prescription drug plan. The plan extends coverage to a segment of the population which does not qualify for coverage under most prescription drug programs. If passed into law, income thresholds for individuals will be $22,000 and $30,000 for couples.

When asked what her most rewarding moment has been in the General Assembly, Vance replied that it is "hard to select the most rewarding, but near the top would be the enactment into law of legislation that I prime-sponsored that I truly believe will help people lead healthier and safer lives." She added that serving as Speaker Pro Tempore also is near the top of her list.

Vance cited Cumberland County Republican Chairman Rick Anderson as someone she is grateful to for his help in her public career, and adds former House member Sam Hayes, Jr., Speaker of the House Matt Ryan, Majority Leader John Perzel and Representative Elinor Taylor to her list as well.

When asked how she has changed since her first election to

the House, Vance replied, "intellectually, I have become aware of many issues and other viewpoints. Also, my self-confidence has increased."

For the 2001-2002 legislative session Vance serves as the vice chairman of the Professional Licensure Committee. She also serves on the Finance, Health and Human Services and Insurance committees.

She hopes to be remembered "as a legislator who had integrity and courage to speak on difficult issues and as one who was a 'straight shooter.'"

Washington, LeAnna M. (D) Philadelphia
Year of first legislative session - 1993

Born in 1945, in Philadelphia, Washington is the daughter of the late LeAnna Washington. A graduate of Lincoln University, she was an employee assistance program manager prior to her service in the House. Washington has three children.

Washington was elected on November 2, 1993 to replace Representative Gordon Linton, who resigned.

In the 1980s she volunteered to work with the Crisis Intervention Network, the 35th Police District and with the Wadsworth Avenue Business Association. She also served two years on the board of Directors for Women in Transition.

Washington was appointed as committeeperson by then ward leader John J. White Jr. in 1980. By 1982, she worked as district office manager for state Senator Joseph Rocks, providing constituent service to those living in the Germantown, Logan, Mount Airy and Oak Lane sections of the city.

Washington then returned to school, and in 1989, she earned a Master's Degree in Human Services from Lincoln University.

A member of the House Select Committee on Non-preferred Appropriations, Washington is exploring ways to reform the way that private hospitals, museums and colleges receive state dollars.

An advocate for the rights of minorities, she has been a member of the Philadelphia Parking Authority, Teenshop, Inc., the National Association for the Advancement of Colored People (NAACP), the Northwest Action Political Alliance, Agape Outreach Ministries, the Lincoln University Alumni Association and Gaudenzia's Eastern Regional Advisory Board.

In the 2001-2002 legislative session, Washington serves as the chairman of the Subcommittee on Public Transportation. She also serves as a member of the Transportation, Insurance and Judiciary committees.

Watson, Katherine M. "Kathy" (R) Bucks
Year of first legislative session – 2001

A former high school English teacher and department head and deputy county administrator for Bucks County, Watson also is a mother who served on the Central Bucks School Board. She and her husband, James R. Watson, have a grown son.

A graduate of the University of Pennsylvania, Watson attended graduate school at Villanova University. She was elected to her school board position in 1985 and also served for several years as a member of the Warrington Township Board of Supervisors prior to her election to the House.

She won her race in the House with a 58 percent vs. 42 percent margin.

When asked what motivated her to run for the House, Watson replied, " as a local elected official, and as a county administrator, I encountered situations, and dealt with issues where the control to solve the problem or the issue was at the state level, not at the county or local level, and I was frustrated by that fact. Running for a House seat would give me the opportunity to bring local and county government concerns to the state level, and have the opportunity to help lawmakers see issues from those perspectives."

101

The obstacles Watson overcame in running "were probably no different that those other candidates experience," she said, adding, "finding enough time, raising money, balancing my job responsibilities with my door-to-door walking campaign."

Watson had considerable support from her family when she ran. "I was supported by my husband and son {Derek}, and also by my extended family: my sister-in-law and her family; my aunt and cousins; and my close family friends," Watson said.

When asked what she considers to be the most difficult challenge facing women candidates today, Watson replied, "Traditionally, it has been difficult for female candidates to raise the level of funding equal to male counterparts. However, both the State Republican Committee and the Bucks County Republican Party financially support women candidates equal to men. There is no distinction. Time is always a problem for any candidate, but it is particularly difficult for women candidates with families that include children."

In advising other women who might run for public office, Watson said, "Get involved in government first at the local level; know your issues and your constituents; and then run for office at the local level, at the state level, and at the national level."

Initially, there may be a difference in the way male members of the House treat their women counterparts. "There may be a wariness," she said, "in dealing with a female legislator. However, once the trust level builds, I think individual differences become meaningless."

Watson believes that some members of the press "still spend an inordinate amount of time observing hairstyles, clothing, makeup and small idiosyncrasies. Some fail to ask substantive questions of women as well," she said.

Citing her mother, Kate McDowell, first in a list of role models, Watson admired her mother's independent spirit and intelligence. She also admires her husband's grandmother, Marie Pittman, for "her strong faith in God and her innate kindness to everyone."

"My father, Jim McDowell and my grandfather, Fred Tempest, gave me the security of unconditional love, and had complete faith in my abilities; they both told me I could do anything I wanted to in life as long as I was willing to work hard and learn all that I needed to do the job," she said.

"Lastly," she concluded, I admire First Lady Barbara Bush, for her humor, her ability to inspire others and her fierce love and support of family."

Watson has chosen the following issues on which to focus as a lawmaker: "affordable health care for all Pennsylvanians; improving educational opportunities and quality of education for all children in Pennsylvania; continuing revision for the Municipalities Planning Code to provide for better management of development and growth at the local level; and (a personal goal), as the former director of the Bucks County Highway Safety Program, to sponsor legislation to further reduce the measurement of the blood level content level to .08 for conviction of driving under the influence of alcohol," she said.

Williams, Constance H. (D) Montgomery
Year of first legislative session - 1997

A champion of women's issues and the Pennsylvania Commission for Women, Williams once was lauded by statewide women's activist Nan Spiers for introducing an amendment to the state budget to increase the commission's budget from $250,000 to $750,000.

"Hooray for Connie Williams . . . for having the foresight and courage to raise the appropriation," Spiers wrote in a letter to the editor of the Harrisburg Patriot News.

Williams, called "Connie" in Harrisburg, was born in 1944 in Long Branch, New Jersey, the daughter of Leon and Norma Wilentz Hess. Married to Sankey Williams, they have two daughters.

A 1966 graduate of Barnard College (now part of Columbia University) with a bachelor's degree in English, Williams earned an MBA from the Wharton School of the University of Pennsylvania in 1980. She serves as a trustee of Barnard College and of the Episcopal Academy in Philadelphia. She is a former trustee of Pine Manor College.

Prior to her House service, Williams was the coordinator of special projects for Congresswoman Marjorie Margolies-Mezvinsky.

Williams, whose uncle was a member of the New Jersey Assembly, defeated incumbent Colleen Sheehan by less than 1 percent in her 1995 election to the House.

"To be heard, raise money and not to sound shrill," are three challenges facing women candidates cited by Williams. She also advised women who are thinking of running for office to "not take politics personally. Have very strong core beliefs and a good understanding of who you are," she said.

When asked if she thinks female legislators are treated differently than males by their peers, Williams wrote, "yes… male legislators can get haircuts and shoe shines {in the Capitol}. The old boy network and cigar-filled rooms still exist, although I suspect women would be welcomed if they could stand it."

Williams cites Congresswoman Mezvinsky and Elsie Hillman, of Pittsburgh, as two of the most admired women in the state. She considers her grandfather as her role model, writing that "he as a consummate politician who cared for people more than for personal power."

The prime sponsor of several resolutions and bills, William's legislation reflects a broad range of issues that are important to her. Bills she prime-sponsored include those addressing the following: prescription equity; transporting children in rear car seats; tax credits for child care expenses; driver's license suspension for non-payment of child support; reproductive rights; and, pedestrian right of way, among others.

When asked about her major issues of concern as a legislator, Williams replied "I believe my core value issues are the important issues of my constituents. They include: quality education, gun control and safety, small business growth with special interest in women in business and safe, affordable child care for all working parents." She also would like to limit the number of bills legislators can introduce and make session schedules more family-friendly.

For the 2001-2002 legislative session, Williams serves on the Education Committee.

Following her tenure in the House, Williams would like to be remembered by the phrase, "she served her constituents."

Youngblood, Rosita C. (D) Philadelphia
Year of first legislative session - 1994

Born in 1946, in Philadelphia, to the late Benjamin and Ruth Carn Moore, Youngblood is the divorced mother of three children and has two grandchildren.

She is a 1985 graduate of Antioch University and the former management improvement supervisor of the Philadelphia Housing Authority. Youngblood also served as a constituent service representative for the Philadelphia City Council and was a credit administrator at Bank Leumi, also in Philadelphia.

She was elected to the House on April 5, 1994, to replace former Speaker of the House Robert O'Donnell, who resigned.

Youngblood served as treasurer of the Delaware Valley Chapter of NAHRO and was a member of Youth Leaders of Philadelphia. Active in Philadelphia civic and community groups, she served on the board of the Korean/American Friendship Society. She also chaired the Friends of Fernhill Park Committee and was a team captain in Operation Town Watch.

The deputy chair of Women in Politics for the Commonwealth of Pennsylvania, Youngblood is active in Parents United for Better School.

Youngblood previously has served on the following committees: Military and Veterans Affairs, Federal-State Relations and Professional Licensure. She also served on the Urban Affairs Committee and its Subcommittee on First Class Cities and Counties.

For the 2001-2002 legislative session, Youngblood was selected as the secretary for the Health and Human Services Committee. She also serves on the Children and Youth and Intergovernmental Affairs committees.

Past Members

Adams, Ella Collier (R) Fayette
1927-30

Adams, the first woman to represent Fayette County, was born in Georges Township in Fayette County, attended the public schools in the county and Beaver College. She was married to J. B. Adams in 1901.

Adams served as an alternate delegate to the Republican National Convention of 1924 in Cleveland, Ohio. Active in political organizations, including the Republican Women of Pennsylvania, Adams also was a member of the "Great Meadows Chapter" of the Daughters of the American Revolution.

A popular Fayette County politician, Adams was "elected hands down" in the second legislative district when, in 1926, she was the first elected woman from Fayette County where the Republicans held a substantial majority. Adams again won a substantial victory in 1928 when the newspaper reported that she was given a "sweeping majority."

Alexander, Jane M. (D) York
1965-68

Alexander was born in Wilkes-Barre on November 10, 1929, the daughter of Isaac C. and Marietta (Fisher) Lehmer. She was a graduate of Dillsburg High School, Dickinson College and Dickinson School of Law.

An attorney who was married to P. Nelson Alexander (1950-1978) and James McHale (1979), Alexander served on the Dillsburg Borough Council, serving as its president for the last two years of her four year term, and on the Northern Joint School District Board. Alexander had four children. She was first elected to the House when she was 34 years old.

A member of the York County, Pennsylvania and American Bar Associations, she practiced before the Orphan's Court and Court of Common Pleas of York County. She shared a law partnership with her first husband and was active in local community groups, including the Dillsburg Woman's Club and the York County Federation of Women's Clubs.

The first woman from York County to serve in the House, Alexander beat Stanley H. Gross, the incumbent, in two elections, the first, in 1964, by a vote of 13,221 to 11,468 and the second in 1966 by a slightly less margin. Gross had previously held the seat for three two-year terms.

When she won in 1964, Democratic State Chairman Oris B. Morse hailed the legislative victory as "a positive vote of confidence in the Democratic Party and its record of accomplishment for the nation, Pennsylvania and York County." He added that the "voters of the district can feel confident that Mrs. Alexander will uphold her pledge to serve their best interests in the General Assembly."

Anderson, Sarah A. (D) Philadelphia
1955-72

A teacher and mother of six, Anderson served 17 years in the House. The daughter of the first black dentist to practice in Florida, Dr. Harry A. and Maude (Smith) Anderson, she was born on January 23, 1901 in Jacksonville, Fla. Anderson was married in 1922 to war veteran and podiatrist, Dr. Adolphus W. Anderson Sr.

Anderson served as inspector of elections, committeewomen and legislative consultant. She chaired the House Joint State Government Sub-Committee on Mental Health and as secretary of the Legislator's Committee on First Class Citizenship. She also was a member of the Democratic State Policy Committee.

A member of the Pennsylvania Historical and Museum Commission, Anderson also served on the Governor's Commission on the Status of Women, his Council on Drugs, Task Force on Human Services, and as a member of the State Advisory Committee on Mental Health/Mental Retardation. She was the recipient of several local and statewide awards and honors.

Anderson was an alternate delegate to the Democratic National Convention of 1956 and a delegate to the national convention of 1960.She was a "respected member of the state legislature and active in Elks and community affairs."

When Anderson died in December of 1992, Jim Nicholson called her "an advocate for the rights of children, minorities, women and the impaired during her 17 years in the state House of Representatives." Anderson began her public career as an elementary school teacher before being elected to represent the 54th district in the legislature from 1954 until her retirement in 1972. She was the first black woman to preside over the General Assembly and serve as a chairwoman of the Health and Welfare Committee, a post she held for four years.

Anderson was responsible for legislation that expanded renal dialysis into neighborhoods with the use of mobile units. She helped spearhead a legislative project to increase knowledge of sickle cell anemia and helped obtain funds to expand mental health facilities and promote the interests of the visually impaired.

Other legislation and political work included sponsoring African-American history activities, a fair housing bill in 1965 and establishment of a junior college in Philadelphia in 1963, that evolved into Community College of Philadelphia.

During an especially tough battle over the income tax in the Legislature in 1971, the Democratic leadership several times sent state troopers to drive Anderson, who was ill, to Harrisburg to vote in close roll calls.

In a political retrospective about the 190th district election in 1966, Elmer Smith wrote that "she was one of us. She lived amongst us, her children went to the same schools we did. She was probably no better or worse than most of us and in that sense she was representative of the people who elected her. The phrase from the election law is that a representative should be 'cut from the cloth of the community.'"

Arty, Mary Ann [Majors]* (R) Delaware
*Married in 1998
1979-88

A registered nurse and mother of three, Arty was born on November 24, 1926, in Philadelphia, the daughter of Henry J. and Pearl Van Dike Scheid.

Arty graduated from the Medical College of Pennsylvania in 1947, West Chester State College (now West Chester University of Pennsylvania) in 1966, and also attended graduate school at the University of Pennsylvania. Arty is a certified health officer and lecturer and is active in several national, state and local health organizations.

A delegate to the Republican National Convention in 1972, Arty was a delegate to the White House Conference on Families in 1980 and appointed a member of the Governor's Council on Drug Abuse the same year.

Shortly following her swearing-in 1979, she was considered "the only health professional in the legislature" and was appointed to the Health and Welfare Committees and to the subcommittee on health. In 1982, she was referred to as the "nurse legislator."

When first elected to the House she unseated a two-term Democratic incumbent, Thomas J. Stapleton, crediting much of her victory to "the great teamwork" of her campaign organizers.

In February of 1979, Arty was one of five Delaware County freshmen to vote against a legislative pay raise that eventually passed.

In 1986, Upper Darby GOP county chairman John McNichol said of Arty, then a candidate for county council, "Women in politics are great incumbents because people don't vote women

110

out... they're very attentive to detail. Men go out and play golf. Women play politics fulltime." Arty won the seat and remained on the Delaware County Council, serving five years as chairman, until her resignation in 1995 to accept the position of County Administrator of Human Services.

At a ceremony recognizing her accomplishments as council member and chairman, a citation was read commending Arty for her "compassion and indefatigable efforts on behalf of the homeless and needy, neglected and abused children and the downtrodden who suffer from the rigors of poverty."

Bentley, Alice M. (R) Crawford
1923-28

The first woman in the United States to preside over a state House assembly, and the first women to serve as a state House committee chairman, Bentley, a single teacher, also was a member of the first class of eight women to serve in the House.

Born April 12, 1859, in Wayne Township, Crawford County, Bentley attended public schools and the Edinboro State Normal School (now Edinboro University of Pennsylvania) from which she graduated in 1883. She taught in the Meadville public schools for several years.

Bentley was elected when she was 63 years old. In 1925, she was the first woman appointed House Education Committee Chairman. She is listed in her biography as having served as a solicitor for several years for the Mutual Life Insurance Company of New York.

While in office she helped found the National Council of Republican Women.

Boscola, Lisa M. (D) Northampton
1995-98

State Senator Boscola was born April 6, 1962, in Bethlehem, the daughter of Richard J. and Anna A. Stofko.

Married to Edward J. Boscola, she is a former court administrator who earned both a bachelor and master of arts degrees from Villanova University in 1984 and 1985, respectively. She worked in the Northampton County Court and as regional director of the Pennsylvania Association of Court Managers.

Boscola served as an "executive on loan" to the United Way campaign and president of the local American Businesswomen's Association. She also is a member of several local business and political organizations.

While in the House, Boscola served on the Agriculture and Rural Affairs, Veterans Affairs and Emergency Preparedness committees.

In March of 2000, reporter Frank Keegan wrote that Pennsylvania's legislative bodies "may be the last formal vestige of entrenched male chauvinist boar hogs in this great land of ours – seven out of 50 senators, 27 out of 203 representatives, a state with a majority female population – {these women} are supposed to sit meekly, act demurely and do as they are told." In response, Boscola said, "Hey, the people did not elect me to be a shrinking violet. I'm not the kind of person who just sits back quietly. OK. So I did grab one Republican leader by the chin once. Look at my record. Sure I shake things up. And I don't cower to the party bosses."

In fact, one of the bills Boscola is most proud of sponsoring is ACT 86 of 1996 the "Motivational Boot Camp Act" which allowed more youthful offenders to participate in boot camp programs. Republican Governor Tom Ridge signed the bill in her district at a ceremony attended by several public officials from both parties.

Boscola was elected to the Senate in November of 1998, in

her final remarks to House members on November 16, 1998, Boscola recalled the remarks of former House member and then U.S Congressman Paul McHale, who said to her "when you get to the House... legislators take one of two paths. The one path they take is they follow their leadership, and they do what they are told, and things are nice. Everybody gets along, and everybody gets along well... but other legislators take a different path. They follow a more independent road, voting for their constituents as opposed to the parties."

Boscola said she could not leave the chamber without expressing to Speaker Matthew J. Ryan "a fellow Villanova graduate - my gratitude and my admiration. You taught me, Mr. Speaker, that your word is truly your bond and that the personal respect for every member and for the dignity of this body are far more important than any political or personal consideration. For that I thank you, and for that I will never forget you."

Brancato, Anna M. (D) Philadelphia
1933-40 and 1945-46

The first Democrat woman to be elected to the House, Brancato was born in Philadelphia on January 17, 1903, the daughter of Joseph and Mary Louise Brancato. A single woman who was an insurance and real estate broker, she was educated at the Academy of the Sisters of Mercy, Banks Business College and Temple University.

Brancato, a Roman Catholic, served as Speaker pro tempore in 1935. She also was the first woman chair of the Committee on Cities, and for two terms, served as the only woman in the House.

A member of the All Philadelphia Democratic Convention, Brancato also served as a member of the Philadelphia Housing Authority in 1936 and as a member of the National Advisory Committee on Woman's Participation in the New York World's Fair, in 1939. She also was active in the following organizations:

113

Susan B. Anthony Memorial; the National Order of Women Legislators; the American Academy of Political and Social Science; the Foreign Policy Association; the Navy League Service; Plays and Players; Pan American Association; the Alliance Francaise.

She also served on the Advisory Committee of the State Council of Defense; the United Campaign; Community Crusade and Red Cross Committees.

Brancato was an alternate delegate to the Democratic National Convention in 1944 and the first woman ever appointed to the Aeronautics Committee of the House.

Brugger, Jeanne D. (R) Montgomery
1965-66

Brugger was a psychologist who earned two degrees from Smith College where she was elected to Phi Beta Kappa, and completed some doctoral study at Harvard University and Bryn Mawr College. She was born on April 12, 1916, the daughter of R.E.A. and Alice R. Griffiths.

Brugger taught psychology and education courses at Drexel University and served as a fellow in psychology at Bryn Mawr.

The mother of two children who was married to John T. Brugger, Jr. also maintained a private practice in psychology.

Active in local and statewide Republican politics, Brugger also worked as a volunteer for several organizations, including such groups as Upper Merion Charities, where she served as director and Colonial Village Women's Association, where she served as president. She was an Upper Merion Township school director for four years beginning in 1961.

While in the legislature, Brugger initiated legislative reforms in special education programs for handicapped children.

Brugger was elected the 15th president of the Medical College of Pennsylvania in 1976. She had been a member of the school's board of corporations since 1965, participating in the college's shift to coeducation in 1969 and its affiliation with Allegheny Health Services in 1988.

Burns, Barbara A. (D) Allegheny
(elected February 15, 1994
vice Thomas Murphy who resigned)
1994

Born in November of 1949, Burns graduated from Chatham College, in Pittsburgh.

Burns won a special election to finish the term of Representative Tom Murphy, who resigned. A legislative assistant who served on the City of Pittsburgh School Board, Burns served only one year.

Carone, Patricia Ann Stone (D/R) Butler
1991-98

The only woman to change from Democrat to Republican, Carone, born on March 21, 1943, in Greenville, the daughter of William Ford and Isabel Gehr Stone. She married Republican Edward H. Krebs on November 1, 1996, while both served in the House. Elected to the House as a Democrat, she changed party affiliation on December 7, 1993. (Krebs also began his legislative career as a Democrat.)

Carone attended Thiel College, graduated from George Washington University in 1967 and Georgetown University in 1974.

She was a delegate to the Democratic National Convention of 1988. While in the House, Carone served as majority chairman of the Higher Education Subcommittee of the Education Committee. As chairman, she held several public hearings and solicited input from the academic, business and student communities and she wrote an extensive two-part text entitled <u>A Report on Pennsylvania's Community Colleges,</u> which outlined 18 subcommittee recommendations to improve community college

115

education. The well-received January 1998 report addressed such issues as funding, outreach, access, participation and student success.

Carone followed up her work as chairman by writing <u>Costs of Postsecondary Education</u> in November of 1998. This 35-page report to the House made recommendations regarding the escalating costs of postsecondary education in the state.

A proponent of set term limits, Carone did not seek reelection in 1998, but rather, retired from the House. In her final remarks before the House, spoken from the Speaker's Rostrum on one of the last days of the session, Carone said, "it is truly amazing how much you have to focus when you know your days are numbered, and it just has helped me a great deal in looking at what I would like to do."

"You have to have a lot of humor in this position … I remember what Matt (Speaker Ryan) said when I changed parties, somebody said, how are you going to deal with her? … and he said, well, he has had root canal work before, and I believe he has probably thought about those root canals he may have had and having to deal with me as well."

Clark, Rita (R) Cambria
1979-80

Mother, teacher and legislator, Clark was born in Johnstown and was married to John J. Clark. They have four children.

Clark graduated from St. Francis College (Illinois), Lock Haven State Teachers College (now Lock Haven University of Pennsylvania), and later studied at the University of Pittsburgh. She is a member of several community and professional organizations, including the Retired Teachers Association, Cresson Lake Playhouse, Community Concerts, League of Women Voters and the Area Arts Council, among others.

Clark also was secretary of the Johnstown Parking Authority

116

and a member of the Johnstown City Council.

Her 1978 victory over incumbent Adam Bittenger, a radio and television newsman, by a majority of 607 votes climaxed a see-saw battle between the two as the returns came in…". Following the election announcement she promised to "work hard for good, honest government."

Clark attributed her victory to "the support of my family and army of volunteers."

She was the second woman from Cambria County to serve in the General Assembly.

Coyle, Josephine C. (D) Philadelphia
1945-46 and 1951-54

Coyle was born in Philadelphia, the daughter of James and Mary Holland Doonan and educated in parochial schools. Active in local Democratic organizations, she also was a community volunteer, having served as captain of the Infantile Paralysis Committee and president of the St. Francis Xavier Unit Alliance of Catholic Women.

A volunteer at the Philadelphia General Hospital, Coyle also taught religion at the Church of the Most Blessed Sacrament and Madonna House. She was married to John F. Coyle and they have five children.

In her 1944 election, Coyle received the most votes of the four candidates running to represent Philadelphia's 10th district. The three other candidates were men.

Crawford, Evelyn Glazier Henzel (R) Montgomery
1955-62

Born on May 9, 1912, the daughter of Howard F. and Edna (Johnson) Glazier, Crawford graduated from Abington High School, Ursinus College, earned a teaching certificate from Temple University and a master's degree from Columbia Uni-

117

versity. She also worked on her doctorate at the University of Pennsylvania.

A housewife, Crawford taught school from 1934 until 1940 and also taught Sunday School for 20 years at Trinity Evangelical and Reformed Church in Philadelphia.

Crawford was a member and past president of the Abington Township Board of School Directors, a member of the board of directors of Ursinus College and served as chairman of legislation of the Montgomery County Federation of Women's Clubs. She also served as the national chairman of Christian Citizenship of the Women's Guild of the Evangelical and Reformed Church in the United States.

Her club memberships include the American Association of University Women (Glenside Branch), the National Federation of Republican Women, the National Parent Teacher Association, Abington Township Association Auxiliary, Abington Civic Club and Ursinus College Women's Club and Alumni Association.

Follwing her election in 1955, Crawford spoke to the members of a local club, the Century Club. In her remarks she said, "to be a good citizen we must know what is going on. We cannot look at legislation only in the light of its effect on us. We must try to see the effect of the action on all of the nation."

She reminded the club members that it is their duty to roll up their sleeves and try to correct situations "not to their liking. Too many persons, she said, stay away from politics because they think politics is "dirty and degrading."

She continued, "each man, at some time in his life, must sit down to a banquet of consequences. We cannot expect we shall get grapes from thorns. As we sit down at that banquet of consequences we will find on the table the sweet with the sour, and the bitter with the good."

She had one son and was the widow of Henry C. Henzel. She later married A. Lowrie Crawford.

118

Crawford, Patricia A. (R) Chester
1969-76

The mother of two and a former legal secretary, Crawford was appointed Deputy Secretary of State in 1978 and served until 1986.

Born September 6, 1928, in Middletown, the daughter of Patrick Farren and Florence Long, Crawford attended West Chester State College. She was married to Robert J. Crawford on June 14, 1947.

Crawford was active in the following organizations: Goshen Grange 121, Valley Forge Historical Society, Legal Secretaries Association, and the Berwyn-Paoli-Malvern Business and Professional Women, who elected her "Woman of the Year" in 1974. She also was an honorary member of the Junior Women's Club of Malvern and the Para Medical Association at West Chester State College.

Other memberships included Green Valleys Association and the Upper Main Line Women's Club.

Even though an incumbent, Crawford barely defeated Democrat John Shea in her 1974 race. She believed "Watergate had an influence on the closeness of the contest as well as Shea's campaign."

Crawford cosponsored major legislation in the field of drug and alcohol abuse, waged a constant campaign for anti-pornography laws. She served as subcommittee chairman of the Health and Welfare Committee.

Crawford served on the Governor's Taskforce to Define Problems of Drug Abuse, the Commission on the Status of Women and was a delegate to the White House Conference on Children.

Denman, Mary Thompson (R) Westmoreland
1931-32

As a wife, mother of two, this attorney was very active in pursing her careers as a lawyer and legislator.

Born on June 1, 1889, in Pittsburgh, Denman graduated from the University of Pittsburgh in 1920. She also received a degree from the university's law school, in 1922. She practiced law in the courts of Allegheny County, the Supreme Court of Pennsylvania and the U. S. District Court. She was the first woman to be admitted to practice law in Westmoreland County.

Denman was active in the following organizations: the Pennsylvania Citizens Council, Pennsylvania Citizens Association and Pennsylvania Public Charities Association. She was a trustee of the Community College of Allegheny County.

As a legislator, she played an active role in the creation of the now named state Department of Public Welfare. She drafted much of the original legislation which created this department. [246] She also was appointed as the first consumer member to the state Milk Marketing Board from 1966-1972. Governor William W. Scranton named her a Distinguished Daughter of Pennsylvania in 1965.

Following her legislative service, Denman served as a legislative analyst for Community Services of Pennsylvania, a nonprofit organization "interested in numerous social service programs."

Considered a pioneer in voluntary health and welfare organizations, Denman was active in the Pennsylvania Public Charities Association, and the Pennsylvania Citizens Association and Council. She was president of the Pennsylvania Conference on Social Welfare.

Her husband, David N. Denman, succeeded her as the elected representative from Westmoreland County. He served in the House in the 1939-1940 session and again in 1943-1944.

Denman died on Sunday, October 19, 1975, in the Polyclinic Hospital in Harrisburg.

deYoung, Rosa Stein (R) Philadelphia
1923-24

deYoung was a member of the first class of women in the House, and the first Jewish woman to serve. She was elected in 1922 and served until 1924. She was married in 1901 to Bertram Issac deYoung, a prominent Philadelphia attorney and art collector, and they had a daughter, Elizabeth.

Born in Baltimore, Maryland on April 3, 1881, she was educated in private schools. She attended Goucher College in Baltimore, and then moved to Philadelphia where she lived for the duration of her life.

After serving in the House, in 1936, deYoung was appointed to the Theater Control Board by Philadelphia Mayor Wilson. She also was on the board of directors of the League of Women Voters, New Hope, a member of the Boards of the Child Study Association and the Planned Parenthood Association.

She died in 1955 at the age of 73.

Donahue, Ruth Stover (R) Clinton
1955-1960

Donahue was born November 19, 1891, in Porter Township, Clinton County. Educated in public schools, Donahue attended Lock Haven Teacher's College and subsequently taught in the county school for three years.

She was vice chairman of the Clinton County Republican Organization for six years and served as president of the local hospital auxiliary. Also, she was a regent of the Colonel Hugh White Chapter of the Daughters of the American Revolution.

Donahue was the vice chairman of Clinton County Council of Republican Women; co-chairman of the Red Cross blood program; and, served on the County Education Committee of the County Unit of the American Cancer Society.

Her husband, Charles E. Donahue, is a former state senator,

serving from 1919 until 1922 and former member of the House, serving from 1939 until 1940.

Duffy, Mary Alice (D) Philadelphia
1957-58

Duffy was educated at Chestnut Hill College where she earned a bachelor's degree in 1950. She graduated from Dickinson School of Law in 1953. She was a member of the American, Pennsylvania and Philadelphia Bar Associations. She also was a member of the Lawyers Club, National Association of Claimants Compensation Attorneys and the St. Thomas More Society.

Following her House service, she and her sister, Sara, opened up a law firm. Duffy & Duffy was formed in 1960 and reportedly was the nation's first women's law firm.

In 1993, Duffy ran for the state Supreme Court but was disqualified from running based on a challenge filed by Commonwealth Court Judge Doris Smith, another Supreme Court candidate. She was disqualified because "numerous signatures on her nominating petitions were invalid, either because the signers were not registered Democrats or had signed more than once."

Durham, Kathrynann Walrath (R) Delaware
1979-96

Durham was born on July 29, 1951, in Chester, the daughter of Glenn S. and Catherine Talarico Walrath. She graduated from Widener University in 1973 and the Delaware Law School of Widener University in 1982.

Durham spent several years teaching Spanish-English courses at Northley Junior High School in the Penn-Delco School District. She is a member of Business and Professional Women, Chester Order of Women Legislators, and the Pennsylvania Export Partnership Advisory Board. In both the 1978 and 1980 elections the young Durham, who ran for the first time when she was 27 years old, defeated Democrat opponent Ralph Garzia by a margin of about 2,000 votes. Garzia, a former mayor and Brookhaven Council member, had served two terms in the House prior to his loss to Durham. She ran against him again in 1986.

In 1988, she defeated Robert Tilghman by a margin of more than 3 to 1, or 17,454 to 5,105. Her opponent in 1992 was a woman, Merry Buffington, and Durham won handily, by receiving over 16 thousand votes vs. 8,696.

During her tenure in the House, Durham chaired the Consumer Affairs Committee and served on the Commerce, Insurance and Ethics committees. She was the sponsor of what was considered one of the most significant pieces of legislation approved in years, the deregulation of electric utilities.

In October of 2000, Governor Tom Ridge nominated Durham to a vacancy on the Delaware County Court of Common Pleas to serve until January of 2002. She was nominated to fill the vacancy resulting from the resignation of Judge R. Barclay Surick, who was named to the federal bench.

Durham has served on the Delaware County Council since 1996. She also practices law in Media.

Dye, Jeanette M. (R) Mercer
1945-1950

The first woman elected to the House from Mercer County, Dye was born in the state of Wyoming, the daughter of John and Mina McOmie. She was educated in the public schools and attended St. John's Hospital of Wyoming and the University of Michigan.

Prior to her marriage to Dr. Ralph W. Dye and the birth of a daughter, she was a nursing instructor. She belonged to Delta Delta Delta Sorority and is a member of Order of Eastern Star of the White Shrine.

She was active in Red Cross work, served as Mercer County

123

Chairman of the Junior Red Cross, district chairman for distribution of food and clothing to needy during the depression, and conducted first-qid classes. She also was a member of the Mercer County Motor Corps, and worked for the County Federation of Women's Clubs and several other organizations.

Farmer, Elaine F. (R) Allegheny
1987-1996

Farmer, born March 14, 1937, the daughter of John R. and Pearle A. McLure Frazier, graduated from Case Western Reserve University, Cleveland, Oh. with a bachelor's degree in business administration. She also earned a master's degree in education in 1964.

Farmer is a former teacher and businesswomen. While in the House, she served on the Appropriations, Liquor Control, Professional Licensure and Policy committees. Farmer served as the chairman of the Subcommittee on Health and Welfare.

The lawmaker was active in the following organizations: Case Western Reserve Alumni Association, corporate board member and trustee at North Hills Passavant Hospital, American Legion Exchange Council, Board of Fellows, University of Pittsburgh Institute of Politics, National Association of Realtors, State Board of Realtors, Greater Pittsburgh Board of Realtors, Andron Epiphanon Fraternity, Theata Phi Omega Sorority, McCandless Town Council, Northland Public Library, North Allegheny Company Chamber of Commerce and Northmont Presbyterian Church.

Some of the awards Farmer received are: Guardian of Small Business 1989-1995, Good Government Award from the North Hills Jaycees in 1988 and Woman of the Year from the North Hills Business and Professional Women's Club in 1988.

Farmer is married to Sterling N. Farmer Jr. and they have two children, Heather and Drew.

124

Fauset, Crystal Bird (D) Philadelphia
1939-1940

Teacher, social worker and civic activist, Fauset is the first black woman to be elected to and the first woman to resign from the House of Representatives. She never completed a term in the House. She also was the first African-American woman in the United States to be elected a state legislator.

Born in Princess Anne, Md. in 1894, she was raised by her maternal aunt, Lucy A. Groves in Boston, Mass. She was educated in public schools and graduated in 1931 from Columbia University Teachers College.

After graduating from college, Fauset became the associate director of the Institute of Race Relations at Swarthmore College for the summers of 1933, 1934 and 1935. She also sat on the Board of Trustees at Cheyney State College.

She was very active in Democratic politics during the early days of the New Deal and was a close friend of Mrs. Franklin D. Roosevelt.

Thanks to her use of the "modern technique" of a strong telephone campaign to reach out to voters and to spread the word about who she was and what she stood for, she easily won her seat. However, she only served for one year before resigning due to her appointment as assistant director in Pennsylvania for the Works Progress Administration, where she was in charge of education and recreational programs. In her maiden speech before the House she asked fellow legislators to show increased interest "in both government and private slum clearance."

In 1941, she was appointed as the special consultant on Negro affairs in the Office of Civilian Affairs in Washington, D.C. Her disappointment with the Democratic Party due to its mishandling of black Americans in the war effort, in 1944, she turned her support to the Republican candidate, and backed Governor Thomas E. Dewey for president. After meeting with Dewey and other Republican officials, she became an advisor to the Republican National Committee's Division on Negro Affairs.

Between the years of 1945-50, she served as an officer of the World Affairs Council in New York. She was a national officer of the YWCA, American Friends Service Committee and American-Korean Foundation. In 1955, the Commonwealth honored her with its Meritorious Service Medal.

Fauset died in Philadelphia on Sunday, March 27, 1965.

Fawcett, Charlotte D. (R) Montgomery
1971-1976

Born on April 20, 1911 in Delaware County, Iowa, Fawcett, graduated from Lamont High School in 1929, and attended Upper Iowa College.

Married to Cecil C. Fawcett in 1930, this mother of two has been a member of several different organizations over the years, including the American and Pennsylvania Library Associations, Huntingdon Valley Women's Club and the Civic Montgomery County Citizens Council. Fawcett also is a former Republican committeewoman and former chairman of the Lower Moreland Township Republican Party.

She was a delegate to the 1967-68 Constitutional Convention.

She won reelection in 1972 because of her "performance in the State House and her integrity." In response to the results of the election that put both the House and Senate in Democratic control, Fawcett said that " it's going to be one big battle from now on. They (the Democrats) have control of both houses and that's a very unhealthy situation. It's better to have one controlled by each party."

Gallagher Ph.D., Sarah McCune (R) Cambria
1923-24

"...one of the first spirited voices for women's suffrage heard

126

in this country, she carried a banner with her friends Carrie Chapman Catt and Susan B. Anthony…"

This was one of the many accolades given Gallagher in a 1954 article of the Mountaineer-Herald. Her file at the Cambria County Historical Society reveals a lifetime commitment to education and civic pride.

Gallagher, a member of the freshmen class of women in 1923, was the first Cambria County woman to serve in the state legislature.

She was a teacher and principal in public, private and normal schools. Gallagher and her sister opened a private academy, a boarding school called Hallesen Place, in Ebensburg to educate "younger pupils" in the social graces. She ran the school from 1904 until 1942.

She graduated from the State Normal School at Indiana with a bachelor's degree in education and later earned a Master of Science degree from the same school. Next, Gallagher went to Cornell University and earned a Bachelor of Philosophy degree. She continued her education overseas by taking classes at the universities of Oxford, in England; Berlin, in Germany; and Sorbonne University, in Paris, France. The University of Pennsylvania awarded her a fellowship in American History, and she completed a Master of Arts degree in 1902.

Gallagher was a recognized authority on Washington, Benjamin Franklin and William Penn. During the time she was abroad, she became the first American permitted to do research at the Library of London, where, at that time, the only history of William Penn was housed.

Prior to opening her school, Gallagher was a professional reader and in great demand as an entertainer both at institutes and in some of the wealthiest homes of New York and Philadelphia. The dress for her appearances was black chiffon over satin, with a deep yolk of real Irish lace. She was large boned, dignified and had unforgettable large gray eyes.

Gallagher is a founding member of the Ebensburg Free Library.

In the legislature Gallagher scoffed at the idea that a "woman's bloc" might exist among her eight colleagues, the first women in the House.

Although she did not chose to run for re-election, Gallagher felt what she had done was enough. "…I ran only the first time because women were given the right to sit and most of them were timid about running. I did it to give them an example." Miss Gallagher died in 1964 at the age of 100.

George, Lourene Walker (R) Cumberland
1963-70

Born in Harrisburg on July 1, 1913, George is the daughter of Lloyd M. and Romaine Senseman Walker George. She attended New Cumberland High School and studied nursing an anesthesiology at Germantown Hospital School of Nursing a Germantown Hospital School of Anesthesia. Before her election to the House, she was a nurse-anesthetist.

George was a member of the Pennsylvania State Association Nurse Anesthetists and the American Association of Nurse Anesthetists.

She also was active in the Business and Professional Women's Club, League of Women Voters, Tri-County Retarded Children's Association, Cumberland County Retarded Children Association, Bosler Free Library, Hamilton Library Association, Cumberland County Multiple Sclerosis Association, Tri-County Heart Association and the American Legion Auxiliary.

George, Margaret H. (D) Bucks
1977-80

Beating all the odds and becoming the first Democrat to represent Bucks County, "Peg" George won two elections due to her well-organized campaign.

128

George twice defeated Robert E. Ferguson, who called her "the great crusader."

When announcing her win in 1978, the county chairman said, "her victory was in great measure, a personal one. We did what we could do to help, but Peg George can take most of the credit herself. She has a lot of people, including a lot of Republicans, who are committed to her. She has put together an amazing organization."

George was born on April 5, 1928, in Chester, the daughter of Margaret Wright Hewitt and Charles H.S. Hewitt. She graduated from Prospect Park High School and Ursinus College where earned a bachelor's degree in 1949.

She was the School Director for Central Bucks and she was a member of the school board. George was a member of the American Association of University Women and the League of Women Voters. She was married to Glenn F. George and has three children.

Gillette, Helen D. (D) Allegheny
1967-78

Insurance agent, accountant, and justice of the peace for Harrison Township, Gillette legislator, mother of three and wife to Michael J. Gillette, Helen D. Gillette played a role in various areas of life. Born in Pittsburgh on March 23, 1919, to Louis Frederick and Georgia Mohn Gillette, Helen served the Allegheny county from 1967-78.

After graduating from New Kensington High School, she continued her education at the University of Pittsburgh. She was a member of Business and Profession Women's Club, Pennsylvania Magistrates Association, National Order of Women Legislators, Women's Civic Club of Allegheny Valley, Community Service Club and Catholic Daughters of America.

Helen Gillette died on November 25, 1991.

Grimes, Helen (R) Allegheny
1923-30

As the first woman elected to the House of Representatives from Allegheny County, Grimes was the first woman to address the House. On February 12, 2000, she read sections of Abraham Lincoln's second inaugural address.

Following her reading at the joint House/Senate joint session President ProTempore of the Senate T.L. Eyre remarked, "I am sure that the Joint Assembly is greatly indebted to Miss Grimes for her participation in the exercises tonight, and I am equally sure that could Mr. Lincoln have been here and heard the lady member of the Legislature deliver his address, perhaps better than he could have delivered it himself, he would have been equally pleased."

Born in Pittsburgh, Grimes was one of the few members of the Allegheny County delegation to remain for Governor Gifford Pinchot's farewell address, which was considered by reporters as scathing.

"Several members of the Allegheny County delegation... left the hall when the governor launched into his harangue on the alleged iniquities of their native county and city, but others remained, and as Representative Helen Grimes put it, 'treated the governor's tirade with silent contempt, which it merited because of its evident falsehood, unfairness and its inspiration in the disappointed political ambitions and personal aspirations which have met with such continuous and dedicated rebukes at the hands of people of Allegheny County,'"wrote one reporter.

Hagarty, Lois Sherman (R) Montgomery
(elected in special election in March of 1980)
1980-92

A former elementary school teacher and first assistant Montgomery County district attorney, Hagarty, in a special election, replaced Representative Anthony Scirica, who resigned.

The daughter of Daniel and Evelyn Wolpert Sherman, Hagarty was born on September 28, 1948. She graduated from Harriton High School, and earned three degrees from Temple University, including a bachelors degree with honors in 1970; a masters degree in education in 1973; and a law degree from the university's school of law in 1973. She worked in the Norristown firm of Wilson, Drayer, Morrow & Furber. She is married to John Joseph Hagarty, Jr. and they have two sons.

Hagarty served as subcommittee chairman of the House Judiciary Committee. She also served on the following committees: Crimes and Corrections; Business and Commerce Committee, Subcommittee Banks and Savings and Loans Associations; and Small Business. She also served on the Pennsylvania Committee on Crime and Delinquency and Task Force on Services to Children and Youth.

Hagarty has been involved in a number of organizations over the years. They include the National Council of Jewish Women and the Women's Advisory Committee, of Montgomery County Community College. She has been recognized with awards from the Greater Conshohocken Chamber of Commerce and several other organizations, including: Friend of Counseling Award, Pennsylvania Chapter of the National Federation of Industry and Business "Guardian of Small Business Award;" and, a "Certificate of Appreciation" from the Pennsylvania Coalition Against Domestic Violence.

Hagarty now serves as a lobbyist in Harrisburg.

Harley, Ellen A. (R) Montgomery
1991-94

Born on December 31, 1946, in Nashville, Tenn., Harley attended Monmouth College in New Jersey where she earned a bachelor's degree in English. She continued her education at the University of Pennsylvania, where she earned a master's degree in city and regional planning.

She is married to Edwin Westbrook Harley.

Harley is a member of the American Planning Association, Urban Land Institute, and the League of Women Voters. She also was appointed by the Speaker of the House to serve a term on the Pennsylvania Council on the Arts and on the Pennsylvania Public Television Network Commission.

Elected into office in 1990 and serving until 1994, Harley co-wrote the Select Committee on Land Use and Growth Management Recommendations, which examined the open space issue in Pennsylvania. Harley also co-authored a study on affordable housing in Montgomery County.

She was a member of the House Health and Welfare, Urban Affairs and State Government committees

Harper, Ruth B. (D) Philadelphia
1977-1992

Harper spent several years as one of Philadelphia's top black fashion models before opening a charm school and running for the House.

While in the legislature, she became well known for her support of women and minority issues. She was the leading force in successfully obtaining state funding for Philadelphia's African-American Historical and Cultural Museum in 1980. She also pushed for the restoration of the North Philadelphia railroad station and state funding for Pennsylvania's neighborhood housing services programs.

Harper fought for $5.3 million in state funds for the "sinking homes" in the Logan section of Philadelphia. The homes had been built on ash and cinder.

Throughout her legislative career she worked for decent affordable housing, handgun control and affordable automobile insurance.

132

Born on December 24, 1927, in Hinesville, Ga., Harper was the daughter of Thomas and Sally Brant DeLoach. She was married to James Harper and they have two daughters.

Harper was educated at Cuyler-Beach High School in Savannah, Ga., Berean Business School, School of Cosmetology, Philadelphia, and also took classes at LaSalle College and the Moore College of Art. She is a graduate of Flamingo Finishing School. She founded and directed her own finishing school, Ruth Harper's Modeling and Charm School.

"In a job where street savvy, influential friends and an instinct for the jugular are often considered requisites for success, state Rep. Ruth B. Harper does it quite well...using charm. Charm, such as one might have learned in, say, the old Flamingo & Modeling School, along with keeping ones knees together, turning with a model's graceful pivot and choosing the most flattering shade of eye shadow. Then again, it's not the usual legislator... she still walks like a model and runs her own modeling and charm school when she's not scrapping over legislation on the House floor in Harrisburg," wrote a reporter.

Harper created the Miss Ebony Pennsylvania Scholarship Pageant, was a board member of the Columbia Branch YMCA, Northwest Branch Red Cross and Women of Greater Philadelphia. She was member of the National Council of Negro Women, Fellowship Commission, Tioga Civic League, the National Association for the Advancement of Colored People (NAACP), the Philadelphia Urban League, Timberly Lake Charities, North Central Women's Political Caucus, and the Democratic Women's Forum. She served as a Democratic committeewoman.

Harper received service awards from the following organizations: Philadelphia Women's Political Caucus, the NAACP, Bright Hope Baptist Church, Philadelphia Tribune Citation of Honor, Variety Club Tent 13, Cosmopolitan Club, Third world 76 Inc. Black Expo and Theate Ne Sorority, Gamma Chapter.

In her 1990 reelection the popular Harper won by a 10-1 cushion.

In a 1981 House debate about cutting off state funds for nearly all Medicaid abortions, an enraged Harper, with a coat hanger in her hand, said, "some men here today would like to see women revert to the coat hangers and back alley abortions. Wealthy women have been able to pay for their abortions and preserve their health. Poor women have to revert to the coat hanger that I am holding in my hand." Hours later the measure passed.

Following her retirement from the House, Speaker K. Leroy Irvis said of Harper, "I congratulate them (those who elected Harper) for sending a woman to the House of Representatives who understood so clearly that she was their voice."

Heiser, Loraine (R) Allegheny
1981-82

Home economist, dietitian, teacher in the Chicago public schools and wife and mother, Heiser was born in Chicago, Ill., on April 20, 1928. She graduated from North Illinois University with a bachelor's degree in 1949. She is married to Richard Hinchcliff Heiser and they have two children.

An active member of her community, Heiser belonged to the following organizations: Zonta, Executive and Professional Women; Alpha Psi Omega (honorary dramatic fraternity); past president of the board of the Women's Center of the North Hills; past president of the North Hills-McKnight Branch, American Association of University Women; and, the League of Women Voters

A delegate to the Governor's Conference on Libraries, Heiser was vice chairman of the North Hills School District Community Advisory Council and a board member of the Women's center and Shelter of Greater Pittsburgh.

Heiser served as the chairman of the Ross Township Republican Party, Chairman of Dick Thornburgh for Governor Campaign of Ross Township, co-chairman of the Allegheny Republican Leadership Training, secretary of the Allegheny County Republican Advisory Committee, Allegheny County Republican Rules Committee, and an alternate delegate to the 1976 Republican National Convention. Heiser also was a member of the Ross Township Council of Republican Women.

She is the recipient of the North Hills Jaycees Good Government Award and was named "Outstanding Woman of the Year" by the American Association of University Women.

Honaman, June N. (R) Lancaster
1977-88

Longtime Republican party leader and only the second woman to represent Lancaster County in the state legislature, Honaman first became active in the GOP in 1949. At that time she was elected co-chairman of the junior group of the Women's Republican Club of Lancaster County. She later was elected vice chairman of the state Republican party.

Born on May 24, 1920, in Lancaster County, she was the daughter of the late Lester W. and Maude Stauffer Newcomer. She earned a bachelor's degree in fine arts from Beaver. She was married to attorney Peter K. Honaman.

While in office and even before her election into the House, Honaman was active in local, state, regional and national Republican political organizations.

She held the following positions: precinct committeewoman; delegate to the regional and national conferences of the women's division of the Republican National Committee (for ten years); and, delegate to the National Federation of Republican Women.

Honaman was a member of the Governor's Commission on the Status of Women and served on Governor's Task Force on Election Reform. She was a board member of the National Council of State Governments and appointed by the Speaker of the House as a member of Governor's Council on the Arts.

135

One of her greatest achievements as a representative was convincing the General Assembly to adopt the 911 emergency phone number statewide. She was the first woman to chair the Military and Veterans Affairs Committee.

Before completing her final term as legislator, she received the Distinguished Woman of the Year award from the Capitol Hill Council of Republican Women. She was also honored by the Women's Republican Club of Lancaster County and received the Chairman's Award for Outstanding Service from the Lancaster County Republican Committee.

Honaman was a member of Lancaster Tennis and Yacht Club, Sea Pines County Club, the American Association of University Women, the Hempfield Woman's Club, Lancaster Chapter of Business and Professional Women and the Lancaster Tennis Club. Honaman was a volunteer with the American Red Cross, the St. Joseph Hospital Auxiliary, and the United Way and Lancaster Airport Building Fund.

Honaman died on Saturday, December 3, 1994. In her obituary she was remembered by friends and fellow legislators as "an honorable and straight-talking public servant who stayed close to her constituents and avoided public mudslinging."

Former Republican legislator Marvin E. Miller said, "she was a devoted citizen with remarkable energy, intellect and humor that complemented her understanding of community issues... she was a gracious lady who always had a thoughtful comment."

Horting, Ruth Grigg (D) Lancaster
1937-38

The first woman elected to the House from Lancaster County was born in January of 1900. She graduated from Millersville State Teachers College in 1920. While a student at Millersville, she was the editor-in-chief of the senior class publication "Touchstone" and was a member of Inter-Scholastic Debating Team.

The lawmaker and cabinet member was the daughter of J. Edgar and Annie Powell Grigg and was married to John Francis Horting. They have a son.

She was an elementary school teacher and community volunteer who loved music. Active in music, religious organizations and women's clubs, Horting was elected president of the Four County Women's Missionary Society and the third president of the Lancaster Federation of Women's Clubs.

Horting resigned from her appointment to the Board of Trustees for the Thaddeus Stevens Industrial School when she was elected to the House. She was one of two women representatives serving in the 1937-38 legislative session.

While in office, she served on the Agriculture, Education, Public Welfare and Cities and Public Health and Sanitation committees.

Her involvement in politics did not end with her term in office. She was vice-chairman of the Lancaster County Democratic Committee and vice-chairman of the Pennsylvania State Democratic Committee, Democratic National Committee's Speakers' Bureau (Women's Division), and attended the Democratic National Conventions of 1940, 1944, 1948, 1952 and 1960.

In 1955, she was appointed by Governor George M. Leader to the cabinet position, Secretary of Public Assistance, an office and department she helped create while a legislator. When the department was combined with the Department of Welfare, she became Commissioner of Public Welfare and was appointed as Secretary of Public Welfare in 1959 by Governor David M. Lawrence for a four term.

In 1963, Horting both was named a Distinguished Daughter of Pennsylvania and received an honorary Doctorate of Humane Letters from Gettysburg College.

Horting has served as citizenship chairman of the Lancaster County Federation of Women's Clubs, was a member of the board of the YMCA and an ex-officio delegate to its Welfare Council. She also was active in the General Federation of

Women's Clubs and the National Federation of Music Clubs.

Horting's concern for the elderly led her to become a co-founder in 1949 of the Lutheran Services for older people in Lancaster, now known as Lutheran Social Services-East Region.

She died on October 10,1988 at the age of 88.

Jones, Frances R. (D) Philadelphia
(elected May 19, 1959 vice Granville Jones, who died)
1959-1966

Elected to the House in a special election, Jones replaced her husband who died on March 7, 1959. Granville Jones had served for 10 years before he died.

According to her obituary, she was born in Waverly, Va. on May 18, 1911. The Pennsylvania Manual, however, lists Mt. Holly Springs as the site of her birth. She was the daughter of the Reverend and Mrs. Walter R. Ward and attended public schools in Milton, later moving to Philadelphia. She had four children.

Jones died on June 4, 1985.

Kelly, Anita Palermo (D) Philadelphia
(elected Nov. 5, 1963 vice William J. Kelly,who died)
1963-78

Kelly was elected to fill the vacancy left by her deceased husband, William J. Kelly, who died on October 27, 1943, while in office.

Born on July 27, 1913, and raised in Long Island, New York, Kelly attended public and parochial schools in Long Island. She studied abroad, majoring in Italian studies and interior decorating in Palermo, Italy.

Kelly was a currency counter for the Federal Reserve Bank for 13 years. She also served on the 34th Ward Democratic Executive Committee, as chairman of the credential committee of Women's Democratic Club and was a member of the board of governors of the American Committee on Italian Migration.

While in the House she served on the following: Health and Welfare Committee, Subcommittee on Health; Investigating Committee on the Issuance of Horse Racing Licenses, Professional Licensure Committee; Consumer Protection Committee (where she served as secretary); and, the Joint State Government Committee Task Force on State Licensing of Professions and Occupations and Human Services.

Kelly a benefactor for 25 years of Saint Mother Cabrini Orphanage and St. Ignatius Home and Regina Home for the Aged.

Kelly was active in the Pennsylvania Federation of Democratic Women and sat as a Trustee on the Board of Directors for the Center for Child Guidance.

In recognition of Kelly's outstanding public service she received the following awards: "Meritorious Award" from the 34th Ward Democratic Executive Committee in 1967; "Humanitarian Award" in 1968; a "Certificate of Achievement" from the Pennsylvania Federation of Business and Professional Women's Clubs in 1968; an "Award of Merit" for outstanding achievement in the field of legislation; and, was the first woman recipient of the "Man-Of-The-Year" Award, given by the Max Slepin American Legion Post 896 for her "untiring and devoted effort on behalf of her community." She was decorated by the Italian Consul General with the Star of Solidarity with the title of "Cavaliere" to recognize her "constant activities aimed at bringing prestige to the Italian name in this country."

Kernaghan, Mae Winter (R) Delaware
1957-70

Kernaghan was born in Philadelphia, the daughter of Arthur

C. and Elizabeth Benckert Kernaghan. Following her graduation from public high school, she attended the Philadelphia Secretarial School. She was married to Frank J. Kernaghan and they had one son

Kernaghan served as vice chairman of the Young Republicans for eight years, state Committeewoman from Delaware County for 10 years, vice chairman of the Republican Executive Committee for 6 years and an alternate delegate to the National Republican Convention in Chicago in 1944.

Other activities she was involved in include: serving as secretary of the Salvation Army Maintenance Campaign Office of Delaware County; president of Yeadon Public Library; member of the Business and Professional Women, district chairman of legislation; Camp Sunshine Board of Directors; president of the Delaware County Parks and Recreation Board; a member of the Yeadon American Legion Auxiliary, serving as its Public Relations Director, president of both the Yeadon Woman's Club and the Women's Federated Club of Yeadon; and member of the Advisory Committee for Public Assistance for the Yeadon Presbyterian Church.

Kernaghan received a citation from the Veterans of Foreign Wars in the United States from the Delaware County Council and was elected to the Pennsylvania Young Republican Hall of Fame in 1963. She also received the Business and Professional Women's "Woman of Year Award" for women in government.

Kernaghan aided the Red Cross Canteen and Prisoner of War Packing Service during World War II and was active in Salvation Army work, serving as director of the local campaign office from 1944 until 1955 and later was director of its Service Office in Delaware County.

Kernaghan died on September 29, 1980, at the age of 79.

Kernick, Phyllis T. (D) Allegheny
1975-80

Phyllis Kernick was born in Penn Hills, Pennsylvania. She attended Penn Hills High School and graduated in 1942. She earned a degree from Robert Morris Business School in 1943. She also attended Point Park College, Duquesne University and the University of Pittsburgh. Kernick was married to William A. Kernick, V. M. D., and they had six children. She was elected as Penn Hills auditor in 1965. She also served as the Penn Hills treasurer in 1969 and 1973.

Kernick was a member of the following organizations: Allegheny County Hospital Development Authority, Allegheny Regional Planning Council, Governor's Justice Commission, Pittsburgh League of Women Voters Penn Hills Chapter, Penn Hills Chamber of Commerce and the Penn Hills Service Association. She also is a life member of the Allegheny East Mental Health and Mental Retardation Center, Inc.

Also, she is active in the Western Pennsylvania Conservancy, Penn Southwest, Camp Shining Arrow, National Order of Women Legislators, Alliance for Consumer Protection, Citizens for Responsible Government and the Turtle Creek Watershed Association.

In 1977, Kernick was presented with the Penn Hills Chamber of Commerce "Citizen of the Year" award.

In her 1978 bid for the House, Kernick was endorsed by the Pittsburgh Post-Gazette.

Following her election, she was the only women in the Allegheny County delegation of 28 legislators, and one of 10 women in the House sworn in, in January of 1979.

Kirkbride, Mabelle M. (R) Montgomery
1929-32

The first woman elected to the House from Montgomery County, Kirkbride was born in Lancaster, Mo. on February 12, 1889.

She graduated from Mrs. Smallwood's School in Washington, D.C. and from the Kirksville, Missouri Teachers' College. Kirkbride taught English in the Kirksville, Mo. High School.

She was married to Dr. Harry Carson Kirkbride in 1910 and they had three children.

When Kirkbride moved to Norristown, she became involved in Montgomery County politics. She is credited with organizing the Montgomery County Council of Republican Women.

Kirkbride was appointed a trustee of the Mothers' Assistance Fund in 1927, was vice chairman of the Montgomery County Republican Committee, president of the eleven combined Mothers' Clubs of Norristown, board director of the Young Womens Christian Association, and a member of the executive board of the Valley Forge Chapter of the Daughters of the American Revolution-United Daughters of 1812.

Kitchen, Shirley M. (D) Philadelphia
*(special election, vice
Alphonso Deal, who died June 3, 1987)*
1987-88

In her initial elections to both the state House, in 1987, and the Senate in 1996, Kitchen replaced legislators who died in office. She replaced Representative Alphonso Deal in the House and Senator Roxanne Jones in the Senate.

Kitchen "coasted to an easy victory" in her race to replace Deal. A former ward leader and protégé of former city councilman, now mayor of Philadelphia, John F. Street, Kitchen toured her district with a loudspeaker on election day, calling for residents to vote "straight Democratic." Results show that Kitchen received three-fourths of the ballots cast that day.

Born on September 18, 1946, in Augusta, Ga., Kitchen moved to Philadelphia when she was five years old. She earned a bachelor's degree from Antioch University in 1979. She also attended Temple University.

Prior to her election to the House, Kitchen was a ward leader and was director of constituent services for Councilman Street. She also ran a neighborhood social service agency, the Ludlow Neighborhood Advisory Committee.

A civil rights and community activist, Kitchen often demonstrated for causes in her district, one of the poorest in Philadelphia. While a member of the House, in 1988, she joined in an angry protest against the illegal dumping of trash and construction debris onto an empty lot two blocks from her house.

Kitchen lost her seat in the House to W. Curtis Thomas, who still holds it. When she was picked to run for the Senate, the Philadelphia Inquirer reported that "one of the biggest prizes in Philadelphia politics this year was bestowed yesterday on a one-time welfare mother who later served in the state legislature and now is an aide to the city council president. The vote was a virtual ticket to Harrisburg for Kitchen."

Kooker, Margarette S. (R) Bucks
1955-66

Kooker, housewife, businesswomen, committeewoman-turned-legislator was active in politics from the time women were granted the right to vote. She was the first woman legislator from Bucks County.

She was born on April 10, 1896, in Harrisburg. She attended public schools in Harrisburg and graduated from its Central High School in 1914. Kooker worked as a secretary for the Bethlehem Steel Company in Steelton.

Kooker was elected to three terms as committeewoman, was

143

a member of the executive committee of the Republican Party in Bucks County, and a member of the county Republican finance committee. She also was a member of the National Organization of Women Legislators. In addition, she helped her husband, Howard Kooker, Jr., with their furniture business, The House of Fine Furniture. The Kookers had one daughter.

Kooker also was involved in many areas of the community, including serving as president of the American Legion Auxiliary of Quakertown and director of the American Red Cross.

She served as secretary of the Bucks County Council of Republican Women, was an honorary director of that Council, vice president of the North Penn Council of Republican Club, served two terms as committeewoman of the Third Ward of Quakertown, was the legislative chairman of the Bucks County Federation of Women's Clubs, co-chairman of the legislative committee of the Quakertown Woman's Club and the national defense chairman of the American Legion Post Auxiliary No. 242.

While serving in the House Kooker was named chairman of the Public Health and Welfare Committee, served as the governor's representative to the White House Conference on Aging and was a member of the governor's Hospital Study Commission. Among her several awards are one for "Outstanding Woman in Public Affairs in 1957, "Who's Who in American Women" and installation as a member of the "Hall of Fame of Young Republicans."

In her response to a 1962 candidate's questionnaire, Kooker offered the following answer to a question about financing "our expanding state services:"

"First of all I would exercise every economy possible to reduce the cost of government. I would staff the Departments with qualified personnel at adequate salaries and expect their services to be commensurate with their salaries. I would have every effort exerted to see that all taxes due the Commonwealth are collected and turned into the Treasury such as collection of the sales tax. I would try to avoid, at this particular time, any further taxation, if at all possible, upon the people of the Commonwealth."

Kooker died at the age of 93 at Quakertown Community Hospital, on March 2, 1990.

Langtry, Alice S. (R) Allegheny
1985-92

Born on June 29, 1932, in Massachusetts, Langtry graduated from North Quincy High School. She attended Boston College and also took classes fromThe Pennsylvania State University and the Community College of Allegheny County.

Married to Alfred Leigh Langtry Jr., they have three children.

Langtry was a member of the corporate administration of Pennsylvania's Elected Women's Association, the League of Women Voters, the Traffic Safety Board of Upper St. Clair Township, the Principal's Advisory Commission of Upper St. Clair High School, and served as a county committeewomen.

She was past president of the Arts Council of Erie; an Upper St. Clair Township Commissioner, who served as the chairman of the Budget & Finance Committee; delegate to the South Hills Area Council of Governments; and, a member of the local Rotary Club.

Langtry is the recipient of several awards, including the 1989"Advocate of the Year" designation from the Library Association of South Hills "Republican of the Year" designation from the Upper St. Clair Republicans, also in 1989.

Leiby, Mary E. (D) Lehigh
1955-56

Leiby was born in Allentown Pa. She was educated in the public school system and graduated from Muhlenberg College 1924. She earned a master's degree from at Columbia University in 1925.

The following year, she was assigned to teach at Allentown's Central Junior High School. Never married, Leiby taught at this school until she retired in 1954, the year she was elected to the House.

Leiby was president of the Women's Democratic Club of Lehigh County.She also was active in the following organizations: the Ladies' Auxiliary to the Lehigh Democratic Club, Women Teachers' Club, Lehigh Art Alliance, Allentown Educational Association, Pennsylvania State Educational Association, National Education Association of the United States, and the Lehigh County Retired Public School Employees' Association.

Leiby died in January of 1978.

Lewis, Marilyn Stoughton (R) Montgomery
1979-82

Housewife, den mother and licensed pilot, Lewis served two terms in the House and left to follow her husband, Drew Lewis, to Washington, D.C. where he served in President Ronald Reagan's cabinet as Transportation Secretary. Her husband also ran for governor of Pennsylvania.

Lewis was born on July 19, 1931, in Philadelphia. She graduated from Norristown High School and attended Harcum Junior College and the University of Miami.

A board member for Senior Adult Center, Lewis taught Sunday School at the Central Schwenkfelder Church. She was also an alternate delegate to the 1976 Republican National Convention and a Republican committeewoman.

Lewis was appointed by the Speaker of the House as a member of the Governor's Council on the Arts.

Following her second election Lewis reported that she relied heavily on her record as a freshman representative in her campaign. She was elected shortly after the incident at Three Mile Island, and made it part of her platform.

She said "I am not against nuclear power, but I am for strengthening regulations concerning the construction and operation of plants, and the disposal of waste." Lewis said she wanted the state and nation to "push forward" on the use of coal as a primary energy source.

MacKinney, Sarah Gertrude (R) Butler
1923-24

The first woman to be appointed to a House committee, MacKinney was born in Chicora, Butler County and educated in the Butler public schools. She graduated from Grove City High School in 1898 and Grove City College in 1898. She taught in the public schools of Crawford, Mercer, Butler and Allegheny Counties.

A librarian for six years at Grove City College, Mackinney, in 1909, entered the manufacturing business.

Mackinney served as the president of the Women's Club of Butler and vice president of the 14 county southwestern district of the state Federation of Pennsylvania Women. She served as the county chairman in Library Loan drives, was a member of the Butler Board of Trade and was elected treasurer of the Carnegie Public Library of Butler.

MacKinney worked for women's suffrage and was a founder of the League of Women Voters in Butler County. MacKinney was the first woman candidate to seek a state office in Butler County.

"Butler's first woman candidate for a state office took the lead at the start of the returns and kept it," wrote a reporter. There is an account of MacKinney's first day in the legislature in the "First Women in the Assembly" section of this book.

Maine, Constance G. (D) Crawford
1987-90

Born on October 28, 1942, in California, Pa., Maine is a graduate of California of Pennsylvania High School. She attended California State University for two years before transferring to Indiana University of Pennsylvania where she earned a bachelor's degree in education. She did graduate work at the University of Pittsburgh, Penn State and completed her master's degree in 1966 at Indiana University of Pennsylvania.

Married to Gary D. Main, they have six children.

Maine was a consultant, counselor and lecturer before her election to the House. She was a member of ZONTA International Business and Professional Women's Club, the National Educational Association, the National Association of Female Executives, and the American Society of Professional Consultants.

She also belonged to the following organizations: Peace Links, Gray Panthers, Farmer's Union, Pennsylvania Elected Women's Association, Capitol Hill Democratic Women's Club and Crawford County Democratic Executive Committee.

Maine is author of two booklets, "Tornado Aftermath" and "Starting Up: Tips for Beginning Businesswomen."

In her first run in 1986, "Maine did something that hadn't been done for 71 years-" she won the state House seat for Democrats. After winning by over 3,000 votes, she said, "I think that people really are tired of the way things are. It's like going through that period of disbelief, and then finally facing the fact that what's being done isn't doing it, so they're thinking that it's really time to try a whole different approach."

In her second election to the House Maine defeated opponent Jim DiMaria, Mayor of Meadville, by almost two to one.

Markley, Marian E. (R) Lehigh
1951-68

"The Lady From Lehigh," as Markley was nicknamed, was the first woman to represent Lehigh County in the state legislature. She also was the first woman legislator to be appointed as chairman of the House Standing Committee on Motor Vehicles and Highway Safety. In 1967, she was appointed chairman of the joint State Government Commission, the first woman in the United States to head such an agency.

The daughter of Edgar and Bertie (Berlin) Hall, Markley was born in Treichlers. She graduated from Northhampton High School and worked as an office manager in private industry for 15 years. She was married to Franklin H. Markley.

Markley was the secretary to House Speaker and Majority Leader Franklin Lichtenwalter during the 1943 and 1945 sessions. She served as an administrative assistant to the Speaker in 1947.

As a legislator, Markley introduced bills that created a process for registering physically disabled electors, benefited emotionally disturbed children and provided education for exceptional children.

Markley served as a member of the Republican County Committee for twelve years, Lehigh County Council of Republican Women, Allentown Quota Club, Business and Professional Women of Emmaus and Macungie, Lehigh Valley Guidance Clinic and the Governor's Committee on Children and Youth. She was the chairman of American Cancer Society and trustee of Lehigh Valley-Delaware Valley Cystic Fibrosis Foundation.

Appointed as a member of the Governor's Commission on the status of Women, Markley also was named a Distinguished Daughter of Pennsylvania in 1957.

Upon retiring from the legislature, she received the "Woman of the Year" award from the Pennsylvania Federation of Business and Professional Women's Clubs. She also was honored

149

by the Allentown YWCA for "distinguished service to the community and society." Markley was a member of the board of Cedar Crest College, and that institution awarded her an honorary Doctor of Laws degree in 1966.

Markley died in Allentown on January 27, 1986.

McCosker, Henrietta C. (R) Philadelphia
1947-48

McCosker, the widow of Joseph R. McCosker, is the mother of M. Joseph McCosker, former director of the Atwater Kent museum.

Born in Philadelphia, McCosker was educated in the public schools of Philadelphia. For eight years, she served as a clerk in the Philadelphia office of the Internal Revenue Service. Later she served as a probation officer of the juvenile court and then was appointed supervisor of juvenile accounts in the Municipal Court of Philadelphia.

The fact that she was active in the Republican Party all her life is reflected in her memberships and leadership positions in the following organizations: the Republican Business and Professional Women's Club of Philadelphia; board of directors of Women's Republican Club of Pennsylvania; Pennsylvania Council of Republican Women; president of the 24th Ward Women's Republican Organization; and, was elected vice president of the Congress of Councils affiliated with the Pennsylvania Council of Republican Women.

McCosker served as a Council of Defense and Air Raid Warden during the war, was a member of the national American Red Cross, and served as the chairman of the 24th Ward Salvation Army Campaigns from 1909 until 1947. She was secretary of the Ladies Auxiliary No. 122 of the Knights of St. John and a member of the House of Good Shepard Auxiliary.

During her one session in the House McCosker sponsored

the legislation creating the Philadelphia Youth Study Center. In 1964, McCosker died in Philadelphia at the age of 79.

McHale, Katherine Pecka (D) Lehigh
(elected May 21, 1992 to replace her husband Paul McHale, who resigned to successfully run for the U.S. Congress)
1991-92

Elected to the Pennsylvania House of Representatives in a special election in 1991, McHale took the seat of her husband, who served in the House from 1983 until 1991 and was elected to the U.S.Congress. They have three children.

Born in on June 27, 1955, in Othello, Wash., McHale graduated from Whitworth College in Spokane Wash. earning a bachelor's degree in Communicative Arts. She later earned a master's degree in telecommunications at Kutztown University.

McHale joined the U. S. Naval Reserves and served with Combat Logistics Group Two, Detachment 204, Script-Tech Communications where she served as a communications specialist as a writer and video producer.

McHale was a member of the Audio Visual Management Association and the International Television Association. She was a member of the boards of directors of the League of Women Voters of Allentown, Bethlehem Musikfest Association, Burnside Plantation, Inc. and an advisor to the Turning Point of the Lehigh Valley organization. She also was a member of the Lehigh County Democratic Committee.

McHale is the recipient of the Society of Professional Journalists Award and the International TV Association Award

McHugh, Connie Black (R) Philadelphia
1991-92

McHugh was born on December 8, 1938, daughter of Archie

151

and Florence Nelson Black. She was a graduate of Hallahan High School in Philadelphia.

She was a member of the Mayor's Commission Women, president of the Pennsport Civic Association and a member of the Capitol Area Council of Republican Women in Government. McHugh received the Pennsport Civic Award for Dedication, E. D. M. Athletic Association Award for dedication service and was named Stouffers Citizen of the Year in 1973.

In the 1970's, she led the fight against a planned ramp to Interstate 95 at Front Street, successfully arguing that an increased amount of traffic would disrupt the residential neighborhood. The ramp was moved to another street. She also helped secure funding for the Ralph Rizzo ice rink at Front Street, was a founder of the Mummers Museum and raised money for low income senior citizens.

Prior to her House service, McHugh was appointed court crier for the Court of Common Pleas, where she worked for 20 years. Her position in the court led to her involvement into politics. She campaigned for Mayor Frank L. Rizzo and she also ran for Philadelphia City Council, losing a "bitterly fought race in 1987 to James Tayoun by 134 votes." In her campaign McHugh had charged that Tayoun was less than honest. Four years later he was sentenced to 40 months in jail for racketeering and tax evasion.

In her 1990 House race she defeated incumbent Democrat Joseph Howlett, becoming the first Republican in many years to win a seat in south Philadelphia. In accepting the nomination to run against Howlett, McHugh quipped that she was not "a kamikaze pilot. We've looked at the numbers, it's very winnable, and I see South Philly going Republican."

In 1991 McHugh filed a court action to clean up the elections. She found that in two elections the previous year absentee ballots were registered for at least three dead people who supposedly lived at a nursing home in south Philadelphia. Two of those registered Democrats had been dead for three years.

After finding out that the nursing home had no more than eight seniors residing there, McHugh began examining the names of 45 other individuals – some of whom are deceased – whose names appear on the city voter lists as residents of the center. When she lost her 1992 bid to return to the House, she blamed the loss on Democratic Senator Vince Fumo, and his "good old boys network" which called her "anti-Philadelphia" for voting against a state budget that provided Philadelphia with millions of dollars. "I'm a thorn in his {Fumo's} side. They torment him in Harrisburg. They tease him. They tell him 'if you're so powerful, how come McHugh beat your guy last time?' I may not have degrees coming out my ears like he does… but I'm not a moron." Fumo ally and City Councilman James F. Kenney once called McHugh the "Princess of Plagiarism" in a letter to the editor.

In 1993, she was named as legislative assistant to State Representative John M. Perzel and later that year she returned to the Philadelphia municipal court system as a trial commissioner.

McHugh died on September 20, 1997.

Miller, Beatrice Z. (R) Philadelphia
1957-60

Born on April 1, 1892, in Philadelphia, the daughter of Edward Zillner and Eva A. Bell, Miller was educated in the public school system at the Regent Academy Girls' High School. She continued her education at the University of Pennsylvania where she studied French and political science.

Miller served as president of the Independent Republican Women of the 22nd Ward and served on the Republican State Committee from 1950 until 1956.

A member of the Pennsylvania Board of Motion Picture Censors from 1939 until 1955, she also was a member of the Hannah Penn Chapter of the Daughters of the American Revolution, the

Philadelphia Regents Club, Professional and Business Women's Republican Club and the Stephen Decatur Chapter of the Daughters of 1812.

Miller served on the boards of the Women's Auxiliary of the Salvation Army, Philadelphia Federation of Women's Clubs and Allied Organizations and Booth Memorial Hospital.

Married to Harry B. Miller, they had two children. Miller died in 1975.

Monroe, Susie (D) Philadelphia
1949-68

Monroe died at age 89, the oldest female member of the House to die in office.

Monroe was born in Jacksonville, Fla. on March 4, 1879, the daughter of Sandy and Susan King Wallace. She graduated from St. Athanansius High School. Monroe was married to James Talbott Monroe and was a dressmaker and beauty salon owner.

She served as a committeewoman and chairman for several years in the 32nd Ward. Monroe was president of the Democratic Loyal Woman's Club, a volunteer for the Infantile Drive of the March of Dimes and the Salvation Army.

The lawmaker was the center of a controversy in late 1967. In a 1993 commentary about blacks and elections, Philadelphia Inquirer columnist Claude Lewis discussed double-dealing and manipulation in American politics. He described the incident when he wrote that he "stood on the floor of the Pennsylvania House and witnessed a very strange event: A one percent increase in the state sales tax – from 5 to 6 percent – mysteriously rode in on the vote of Rep. Susie Monroe, a Philadelphia Democrat. Trouble was, Monroe was back home in her sick bed. I called to tell her the news, and it almost finished her. No politician ever admitted pulling the lever in Monroe's absence."

154

Monroe was memorialized in House Resolution No. 287 which passed unanimously on November 12, 1968. It read, in part: "During her tenure in the House she was in the forefront to pass employment for fair employment practices, housing and slum clearance and in public health programs." Monroe had sought to retire at the end of the session.

Monroe died on November 7, 1968 at Temple Hospital.

Munley, Marion L. (D) Lackawanna
(elected September 9, 1947 in a special election to replace Robert W. Munley, who died.)
1947-64

Second only to Rep. Elinor Z. Taylor in years of service in the House, Munley resigned when her district was combined with another Democratic House member's following reapportionment.

Born in Buffalo, New York, on August 19, 1905, the daughter of Martin and Julia Walsh Langan, Munley graduated from Scranton's St. John's High School and Marywood College. She also attended The Powell School of Business.

From her early career in the 1920's, when she served as secretary of the Congressman Boland and "Hoban for Judge" campaigns until after her retirement in the late 1960's, she spearheaded Democratic functions in the county.

Munley's husband, who died suddenly on January 25, 1947, served in the House from 1939 until 1947 and they had two sons, both living in Lackawanna County, attorney Robert W. Munley and Federal District Court Judge James M. Munley. Munley's father-in-law, William J. "Ring" Munley, also served in the House from 1922 until 1938 when he was replaced by his son.

Following the special election when she replaced her husband, Munley went on to win nine more elections. She was the first, and today remains the only women to represent a

Lackawanna County legislative district.

A lifelong Democrat who regarded party loyalty as a major virtue, Munley was an active member of the community in business and civic organizations. She was the organizer and president of the Twentieth Ward Democratic Club and served as secretary of several business and civic organizations in Lackawanna County. She was a leader in the establishment of industry in the northern Lackawanna County area.

Munley was a member of the following organizations: Young Democrats of Lackawanna County, Blakely Democratic Club, Jermyn Democratic Club and the Women's Democratic Club of Mayfield.

She also was a member of the American Legion Auxiliary, Abrose Revels Post No. 328, Archbald Recreation Association, "Girl Scout Committee" of Archbald, and the Archbald Civic Association.

During her tenure in office she was recognized as a leading proponent of labor legislation. Munley was rewarded for her leadership in the House by her peers when they elected her secretary of the Democratic Caucus in 1963.

During her legislative career she also was instrumental in developing the Archbald Glacial Pothole area into a state park and created a number of state highways in her county.

Munley claimed that one of her greatest accomplishments while a legislator was a bill she sponsored and was passed on December 17, 1959 - House Bill No. 66 - which prohibited pay discrimination based on gender.

Following her retirement from the state legislature, Munley's accomplishments culminated in her election, on January 5, 1965, as Secretary of the House.

In her obituary, Munley was remembered as a "legislator who won the respect of her male colleagues, who treated her as an equal. For instance, she once served as secretary of the Democratic Caucus... on a few occasions she was given the gavel and presided over that body."

Munley died in Scranton on September 15, 1983. Following her death her sons presented her oil portrait to Speaker K. Leroy Irvis who hung it in the Speaker's Office.

Odorisio, Helen R. (R) Delaware
(elected in a special election July 7, 1967 to replace Rocco A. Odorisio who died April 5, 1967)
1967-68

Odorisio ran for the House in 1967 to fill the seat left empty by her husband who died before completing his term. Her husband had about 18 months left to serve of his fifth legislative term when he died. Odorisio defeated her Democrat opponent, Shirley Thomas, by a 3 to 1 margin.

The lawmaker's election to the House that year had special significance because the Governor Raymond P. Shafer needed a majority to pass a tax program bill he was proposing, and there was some opposition from fellow Republicans.

At a victory buffet supper at a Radnor restaurant, Odorisio was on the verge of tears when supporters called on her for a victory comment. Radnor Republican Chairman James Merriman presented a bouquet of American beauty roses to Odorisio, who promised to serve her constituents "to the best of my ability" and vowed to follow the policies that her deceased husband would have wanted.

It was suggested to Odorisio by the local justice of the peace that she work for legislation that would eliminate a special election to fill a vacancy caused by death. He said this legislation would enable the county courts to make an interim appointment as is done in other instances, and cited the "economical advantage of such legislation."

Pashley, Kathryn Graham (D) Philadelphia
1955-66

Pashley was born on April 3, 1911 in Philadelphia, the daughter of Francis P. and Irene Minford Graham Pashley. Pashley attended parochial grade school and graduated from Catholic High School of Philadelphia.

Dedicated to the Democratic Party, Pashley spent her life involved in politics, with her interest developing during the presidency of Franklin Delano Roosevelt. She was an ally of political powerhouses William J. Greed and John F. Byrne. Both men helped in her elections through the years.

While in the House Pashley served as vice chairwoman of the House Health and Welfare Committee. This position complimented her volunteer work as vice chairman of the March of Dimes where she led the fight to eradicate infantile paralysis in the state, which led to the requirement of babies to be immunized.

With Representative Mary Varallo, she founded the Women's Democratic Club of Philadelphia. Pashley served as Democratic committeewoman, and during the 1940's, as chairman of the 35th Ward. She was elected to the Democratic executive committee in the 56th Ward.

Pashley was appointed to a number of posts in the Sheriff's Office, the offices of City Council and as an administrative assistant in the state senate.

Pashley was also active in the Longport Civic Association and the Longport Democratic Club in New Jersey, where she became a friend of former Mayor of Philadelphia James H.J. Tate.

She was an alternate delegate to the 1956 and 1960 Democratic National Conventions. Pashley served as captain of the Infantilc Paralysis Campaign. She was the recipient of the Distinguished Service Certificate of the American Legion in 1960.

Pashley died on December 2, 1981 at the age of 70.

158

Pennock, Martha M. (R) Philadelphia
1925-34

Born in Union County in 1890, Pennock attended school in New Berlin, in Union County, and Mahanoy City, Schuylkill County. She was married to William C. Pennock. She worked in the executive offices of N. Snellenburg and Company of Philadelphia. Pennock was elected secretary of the 34th Ward Republican Women's Committee for four years.

She was honored on April 10, 1928 before a crowd of 800 guests at the Hotel Pennsylvania in Philadelphia for "her fulfillment of party obligations while in the state legislature."

Penock was the sister-in-law to Judge Evan Thomas Pennock who was a magistrate for 21 years and a well-known Philadephia Republican Leader.

Pitts, Lillie H. (R) Philadelphia
1923-32

Lillie H. Pitts was born in Hackettstown, Warren County, New Jersey. She graduated from the Wilkes-Barre Female Institute and later from West Walnut Street Seminary in Philadelphia.

Reibman, Jeanette F. (D) Northampton
1955-56 and 1959-66

Reibman's career in the General Assembly began in the House, laying the groundwork to make history as was the first woman to be elected to the state Senate in a general election.

Born in Fort Wayne, Indiana, Reibman is the daughter of Meir and Pearl Schwartz Fichman. She earned a bachelor's degree from Hunter College in New York City and a law degree from Indiana University Law School, where she was one of only two women attending the law school at the time. Reibman was admitted to the Indiana Bar in 1940.

Following graduation, she found a job in Washington, D.C. working with the Director of the Office of Emergency Management, who was a fellow woman lawyer.

During World War II, she was an attorney for the War Department and later for the War Production Board. She married Nathan L. Reibman soon after and moved to Easton, and raised their three sons. She soon became interested in local education and political campaigns.

Through her membership in the American Association of University Women and the League of Women Voters, she became more active in politics. She was interested in running for the local school board, but her husband encouraged her instead, to run for the State House of Representatives.

Reibman was the first woman elected to the House from Northampton County. She was a member of the bars of the Supreme Court of the United States, the U.S. Tax Court and the U. S. Federal Court for the Eastern District of Pennsylvania.

In her first run for the House, Reibman led five men who were in the race for three 2nd district seats.

Reibman lost her bid for reelection to the House in 1956 by only 210 votes and won it back in 1958. She was reelected in 1958 because "she sponsored much humane legislation in her term in office."

During her tenure in the House, she served as secretary on the Welfare and Elections and Apportionment committees. She also was a member of the Judiciary and Boroughs committees. In 1959, she was appointed chairman of the House Education Committee. Reibman also was a member of the Governor's Committee on Education.

Ritter, Karen A. (D) Lehigh
1987-94

Ritter is the first daughter to follow her father into the legislature representing the same district. In 1994, she was the first

160

woman to run for lieutenant governor in the state.

The lawmaker was born on February 28, 1953, in Shirley, Mass., the daughter of James P. and Faye E. Morrissey Ritter. Her father represented the 131st Legislative District from 1964 until 1982.

While serving in the House, Ritter held the leadership posts of deputy majority whip and deputy Speaker Pro Tempore. In addition to her House committee assignments, she was appointed by the Speaker to serve on the Children's rust Fund Board, the Legislative Budget and Finance Committee and the Task Force on Violence as a Public Health Concern.

Ritter was the author of the Pennsylvania Crime Victim's Bill of Rights, which gives basic rights and protection to victims of crime and became law in 1993. She also spent four years – working with a coalition of legislators, prosecutors, advocates and judges – writing comprehensive revisions to the sexual offenses statutes. Her legislation passed the House several times but did not pass the Senate before she left office. However, it was reintroduced by another legislator, passed and finally signed into law in early 1995.

Prior to her House service, Ritter was a member of Allentown City Council from 1982 until 1986.

Ritter served as the chairman of the boards of directors of: Planned Parenthood of North East Pennsylvania in 1993 and the National Abortion and Reproductive Rights Action League of Pennsylvania in 1998-99; and as co-chair of the board of directors of Pennsylvania's Campaign for Choice in 1996-97.

Ritter also was a member of the boards of directors of the following: A Woman's Place, a Bucks County domestic violence shelter program; Community Services for Children, a Lehigh County Head Start Program; Crime Victim's Council of the Lehigh Valley; Turning Point, Lehigh County domestic violence shelter program; Treatment Trends Foundation, a drug and alcohol treatment program; and the Girl's Club of Allentown. She also was a member of the board of associates of Cedar

Crest College, the League of Women Voters of the Allentown Area, the Allentown Women's Club and the Pennsylvania Federation of Democratic Women.

Ritter is the recipient of the following awards: Appreciation Award from the Crime Victim's Council of the Lehigh Valley for her legislative work; Award of Distinction from the Pennsylvania Coalition Against Domestic Violence; Women's Leadership Award from the Allentown YWCA; special recognition from Sexual Assault Prevention and Education Network of Western Pennsylvania; special recognition for Outstanding Support of Girl Scouting from the Pennsylvania Girls Scouts.

Also, she received the Partner in Independent Living Award from the Lehigh Valley Center for Independent Living; Distinguished Service Award from the Pennsylvania Coalition of Citizens with Disabilities; Public Citizen of the Year Award from the Lehigh Valley Chapter of the National Association of Social Workers; Clara Bell Duvall Award from NARAL-PA; and, the Outstanding Alumnus Award from Northampton County Area Community College.

A National Merit Scholar, Ritter graduated from L.E. Dieruff High School in Allentown in 1971. She earned her paralegal certification from Northampton County Area Community College. Prior to her election to the House, she managed title insurance agencies.

Ritter was an alternate delegate to the Democratic National Convention of 1980 and a delegate to the conventions of 1984, 1988, 1992 and 1996.

When she left the legislature, Ritter joined her husband, Robert Wolper, in a company called Wolper & Ritter Associates, Inc. The company provides strategic planning, communications and public relations services to unions and non-profit organizations. They also provide political consulting to Democratic candidates.

Ritter also hosted a weekly radio program, "Working Family Matters," which aired on as many as 25 stations from New York City to Washington, D.C.

Rudy, Ruth Corman (D) Centre
1983-96

Honored several times for service to her community and dedication to the Democratic Party, Rudy garnered political support through her strong ties to the party and her commitment to her constituents.

Born in Millheim on January 3, 1938, Rudy is the daughter of Orvis and Mabel Stover Corman

Consistently endorsed by the National Rifle Association, her campaigns centered on mud-slinging as well as ideological polarization on issues such as abortion, but she won decidedly every time.

While in office, she worked hard for women's issues. In 1989, Rudy proposed and pushed through a bill requiring medical insurance coverage of mammograms for women over the age of 50 and any physician-ordered mammogram for women under 50. The House also passed her "restroom equity" bill - called "potty parity" - which called for a mandate that would cut the time that women spent in restroom lines by adding more toilets in public places.

A former Centre County prothonotary and clerk of courts who helped run a family business, Rudy said that U.S. President John F. Kennedy inspired her to switch to the Democratic Party.

First elected to the Democratic National Committee in 1980, she was a delegate to the Democratic National Conventions of 1980, 1988 and 1992.

She held many prestigious positions within the party, including president of the National Federation of Democratic Women from 1987 until1989.

Rudy was named Pennsylvania Federation of Democratic Women's Woman of the Year in 1982, and Outstanding Democratic Elected Woman in 1992.

That same year, Rudy was criticized because she attended a convention in St.Thomas, a popular Caribbean island, and was reimbursed with taxpayer dollars. The convention, which began

163

only two days after the election, was advertised as much "needed R & R for candidates and legislators." The convention included speakers such as Louis Sullivan, then-U.S. Secretary of Health and Human Services, and seminars on a variety of government-related topics.

In 1996, Rudy ran for the seat of retiring U.S.Congressman William F. Clinger, Jr., of the 5th Congressional District. She ran against state Senator John Peterson, a Venango County Republican. Less than a month before the election, Peterson blamed Rudy for stirring up controversy regarding the senator's treatment of women. Peterson had been accused of sexual harassment, allegations which were almost 10 years old, weeks before the election. Though Rudy denied any involvement in the matter or timing, she did not recover and lost the race.

Rudy attended the Carnegie Institute and Pennsylvania State University. She lives with her husband, C. Guy Rudy, and three children in Centre Hall, Pa.

Rudy may hold the all-time record for legislators and former lawmakers attending national conventions. In 2000 she attended her 8th Democratic National Convention in Los Angeles, Ca. It was the 6th time she served as a delegate. She was a delegate supporting Vice President Al Gore.

Rudy is widely-known at conventions for her wild headgear. At the 2000 convention she wore a garden sprinkling can on her head with a sign that read "Gore sprinkled with growing ideas." At the 1992 convention she sported a hand-crocheted watermelon hat created by her mother-in-law. One of the people who noticed was a curator from the Smithsonian Institution. Museum officials asked if they could have the "Slice of Life" hat for their American politics collection.

Rudy retired from the House to mount her unsuccessful run for the U.S. Congress.

In June of 2000 Rudy was elected to a four-year term on the Democratic National Committee representing the National Federation of Democratic Women.

164

Scanlon, Agnes Ruddock (D) Philadelphia
1977-78

A beautician and business owner, Scanlon was born on December 22, 1923 in Springfield, Mass., the daughter of Robert Henry Austin and Sarah Morton Tweedley Ruddock.

She graduated from the High School of Commerce in Springfield, and completed her education at the vocational school, Flore Institute of Cosmetology. She also studied at the Berlitz School of Languages.

Before becoming a legislator, Scanlon made her living as a beautician, shop owner and teacher of beauty culture, as a tavern owner and an administrative assistant to the Register of Wills.

She served as register of wills, administrative assistant for the Philadelphia Parking Authority and Leader of the 33rd Ward in Philadelphia. She was a member of the Kensington Ramblers Boys Club, a group that named her their 1973 Mother of the Year," the Juniata Park Boys Club, Ascension Catholic Church and the 33rd Ward Democratic Club.

Scanlon is married to Joseph J. Scanlon and they have four children.

Seyfert, Ph.D., R. Tracy (R) Crawford
Year of first legislative session - 1997

A licensed psychologist with degrees from Villa Maria College (B.A.), Edinboro University of Pennsylvania (M.A.) and the University of Pittsburgh (Ph.D.), Seyfert was born in 1941 in Bridgeport, CT. She is the daughter of Lawrence Tracy and Irene Monroe and has two grown children.

Seyfert won her first election by only a 5 percent margin. She won with a whopping 73 percent in 1998.

From 1984 through 1996 she served on the Erie County Council.

When asked if she was conscious that she is a minority in the

165

House, Seyfert responded "not as a female, only in seniority." She believes women are treated differently than males because women just "don't usually have the seniority the males have."

Seyfert major issues included economic development, education reform and protecting individual rights that are guaranteed by the Constitution. She was the prime sponsor of an amendment to make the state Game Commission "more accountable to customer service, program accountability and fiscal accountability." Her greatest accomplishment as a legislator, Seyfert believes, is "obtaining numerous grants for my area and instituting high quality constituent service."

The author of several House resolutions, Seyfert was the prime sponsor of two bills in the 1999-2000 legislative session, one providing for a higher education tuition assistance program for volunteer emergency services personnel. The other added an 11th member to represent Lake Erie in the Pennsylvania Fish and Boat Commission.

Citing her father, her campaign manager and her loyal friends as those who helped her the most in her public career, Seyfert believes that as a legislator she has become "more astute."

Seyfert reports that she would like to be remembered as one who "helped people and communities and made a positive difference."

Following an admission of illegally obtaining federal property, Seyfert resigned from the House in the spring of 2000.

Sheehan, Ph.D., Colleen A. (R) Montgomery
1995-96

This former college professor at Villanova University, was born on January 7, 1956, in Plattsburgh, N.Y., the daughter of John and Ramona Sheehan.

Sheehan graduated from Willsboro Central School in 1973. She earned her bachelor's degree at Eisenhower College in 1977.

She earned a master's degree in 1979 and a doctorate in 1986 from Claremont College.

The one-term lawmaker is married to John A. Doody.

Sirianni, Carmel A. (R) Susquehanna
1975-88

Born September 14, 1922, in Old Forge, Sirianni is the daughter of John and Amelia Pascoe Sirianni.

Sirianni earned a bachelor's degree in business administration, English and social studies from Bloomsburg State College (now university). She earned a master's degree in education and guidance from Bucknell University. She studied further at Penn State and Marywood College. She taught and was assistant principal and guidance counselor for Hop Bottom and Mountain View school districts for 23 years. Sirianni never married.

Sirianni was an administrative assistant to Speaker of the House Kenneth B. Lee during the years of 1967-1974. After he retired, she was elected to his seat and continued to represent the Endless Mountains Region until her retirement in 1988.

She served as vice chairman of the 10th and 11th Congressional Districts for the Reagan-Bush '84 Campaign Committee. She also served as a member of the executive board of the Republican State Committee and was chairman of the Susquehanna County Republican Committee.

Sirianni's district fell victim to legislative reapportionment after the 1980 census. Though her constituency changed, she successfully won reelection in 1982, 1984 and 1986. During her seven consecutive terms as a legislator, she represented parts of Bradford, Sullivan, Susquehanna and Wyoming counties.

In her 1982 race, the newspaper reported, "Representative Carmel Sirianni had no trouble getting more votes than her opponent, Edward Manhertz."Manhertz was the former mayor of Meshoppen.

167

She was a member of the Hop Bottom Civic Club, Hop Bottom Planning Commission, Susquehanna County Republican Women. The lawmaker served on the boards of directors of the Susquehanna County Cancer Society and the Northeastern Pennsylvania Crippled Children's Society.

Speiser, Martha G. (R) Philadelphia
1923-24

Born in Belfast, Ireland on May 15, 1884, Speiser was educated in the public schools of Philadelphia. She married Representative Maurice J. Speiser in 1913, who was then serving in the House. He served as an assistant district attorney.

Speiser was an active member of Philadelphia community, especially in the arts. Additionally, she was the district chairman for the Liberty Loan and did work on Relief and Red Cross drives.

Speiser and her husband were among some of the earliest collectors of modern art. At their home, they hosted many gatherings of musicians, painters, writers and others engaged in the arts. She donated many works of art to museums, including an important Modigliani sculpture to the Philadelphia Museum of art in her husband's memory. She also contributed works to the Museum of Modern Art in New York.

Organizations that Speiser belonged to include: the Art Allliance, the Philadelphia Orchestra Association and the Philadelphia Council of the Performing Arts.

Speiser died at the age of 89 on September 22, 1968.

Telek, Leona G. (R) Cambria
1989-92

The daughter of Joseph Podgorney and Marie Gomulka, Telek was born on April 6, 1931. She graduated from East Connemaugh High School in 1949. She was married to the late

William Telek, a House member who was murdered in May of 1988 while in Harrisburg. They have seven children.

She won her first election by only 703 votes. Many at the time felt that she was elected to the House "on sympathy votes" following her husband's murder. In her reelection, she proved otherwise by defeating her opponent by over 3,000 votes. "Telek, who has seven children and seven grandchildren, said the number 7 was a lucky one for her on election day in her quest for victory in the 70th" district."

Following her impressive win, Telek also said, "we worked hard and we deserve it. All that nonsense they said, that I wasn't qualified, was baloney. I would never say that about anybody..."

While in office, Telek served on the Aging and Youth, Military and Veterans Affairs and Transportation committees.

Both Telek and her husband "built up a positive reputation of being accessible to and helping the voters in their district. That reputation of assisting her constituents, she said, helped carry her on to victory" in her second election.

Telek was a member of the following organizations: Business and Professional Women, American Cancer Society, American Heart Association, 1889 South Fork Hunting and Fishing Club, National Conference of State Legislatures, National Order of Women Legislatures and the Cambria County Historic Society.

Telek was one of three widows in the state House elected to succeed their husbands that term. The others were Jean T. Wilson, a Republican from Bucks County whose husband died of a heart attack in March while vacationing in the Bahamas, and Susan Laughlin, a Democrat from Beaver County whose husband died of cancer in April.

Thomas, Martha G. (R) Chester
1923-1926

Thomas was the joint owner of a 200-acre parcel of farmland which was part of the original tract bought from William Penn by the first Thomas family members to arrive in the colonies.

Born February 13, 1869 in Whitford, Pa., Thomas earned an associate's degree from Bryn Mawr College. A single woman, she was engaged in farming with her sister and brother-in-law. Thomas shared first prize in 'analysis of many samples of milk" at the Chester County farm produce show in 1925.

Thomas served her community through membership in a variety of civic and social clubs. She was a member of the board of managers for the Chester County Hospital, serving as its chairman from 1917 until 1919.

She also joined the following organizations: member, the Women's Committee of the Council of National Defense for Chester County; chairman, Chester County War Loan Organization; vice president of the Pennsylvania League of Girl's Clubs; vice president of the Chester County League of Women Voters; and, treasurer, Pennsylvania League of Women Voters.

In the first election allowing women as candidates in 1922, reporters wrote that "voting was indifferent in Chester County, at least in West Chester section, and general apathy seemed to prevail… only the women seemed active and they did much work in getting out voters, conducting automobiles in true campaign style, while many of them were early at the voting places and cast the first votes. Women supporters of both Republican and Democratic tickets were equally active and as a result early returns indicated that women may figure among the winners."

Toll, Rose (D) Philadelphia
1971-76

Turning from her profession as a registered nurse, Rose Toll entered politics in 1970. She represented Philadelphia's 200th Legislative District for six years, during which she sponsored the Generic Drug Law which allows pharmacists to substitute generic drugs for compatible name-brand drugs.

Born Rose Ornstein on June 4, 1911, in Philadelphia, she married Herman Toll, a state representative who served between 1950 and 1958 and who also served as U.S. Congressman from 1958 until 1966. They had two children. It was through this marriage that Toll's interest in politics developed and spawned a new career.

When her husband died in 1967, from complications related to Lou Gehrig's disease, she assumed his role as leader of the Democratic Party's 50th Ward in Philadelphia.

After winning reelection in 1972, Toll faced a fierce battle in the Democratic primary with John F. White, a popular African-American candidate. The demographics of the district were changing; the racial makeup of Toll's constituency was shifting quickly. She won the nomination in 1974, and the election, but in 1976 she lost the primary to White, even with the support of the Democratic City Committee. White garnered enough support to win the control of the 50th Ward from Toll in 1978.

In 1978, Toll made one final bid for political office by entering the primary for the state Senate seat of the 36th District. In a political maneuver, she tried unsuccessfully to remove her name from the ballot in order to consolidate support behind a single liberal candidate. Both Toll and the candidate she supported lost, ending her political career.

Toll was a member of the Pennsylvania Council on the Arts as well as second vice chairman of the Philadelphia County Democratic executive committee.

Toll died in 1997 of complications of Alzheimer's disease, survived by two sons and six grandchildren.

Tresher, Maud B. (R) Westmoreland
1925-26

Trescher, a career newspaper reporter, wrote a front page story for Jeanette's <u>The News-Dispatch</u> following her first day in the state legislature.

"The battle over the speakership of the 1925 session has been happily concluded without bloodshed or blows, each of which the readers of newspapers might have been warranted in expecting judging from the exciting headlines which have greeted Pennsylvanians for the past week or ten days," she wrote.

Of her treatment by male colleagues, she declared, "oh, they treat us beautifully. They are most chivalrous. They will do everything for you except let you in on their secret conferences. The result of which you finally, after some weeks of experience, learn to gather from the atmosphere."

Tresher was born to William J. and Mary Elizabeth Blair Byers on December 28, 1876, in Hempfield Township, Westmoreland County.

Trescher was educated in the public schools, graduating from Jeanette High School in 1876. She was married to John H. Treschler and they had four children.

Her career began as a reporter for the Jeanette Dispatch, where she met and married her husband in 1898. He was the editor of the paper and died in 1917.

Trescher gave much time to welfare and community work. She was the first woman to serve as school director for the Jeanette School Board, where she was elected to two terms.

Trescher's volunteer work include: president of the Union Aid Association; vice-president of the Westmoreland Chapter Red Cross; member of the Daughters of the American Revolution; director of the Women's Association of Westmoreland Hospital; and, director of Westmoreland Children's Aid Society.

The one term lawmaker was the first woman from Westmoreland County to be elected to the House.

True, Katie (R) Lancaster
1993-2000

To fulfill a campaign term limit promise she made in 1992,

172

True left legislative service in 2000 to become a statewide candidate for auditor general.

Born in 1941 in Baltimore, Maryland, the mother of three and stepmother of three more grown children, True is the daughter of George A. and Henriette Ann Ansel Buck and is married to Peter True. Her husband is an elected committeeman.

Prior to her House service, True served as a party committeewoman from 1990-92. She also was a TELLS tutor and was active in several community agencies, including the National Drug Watch, Kids Saving Kids, Parents Caring About Kids, and others. She is the author of The Substance Abuse Training Manual.

A champion of children's issues before and during her tenure as a legislator, True chaired the select subcommittee formed in the House to investigate the state's protective system. The final report of the committee resulted in legislation passed and signed into law by Governor Tom Ridge.

In advising women candidates, True said to "evaluate carefully your priorities and decide what you want to do with your life. Then, if politics feels right, jump right in!"

True is the prime sponsor of several bills, including the Breast Cancer State Tax Check-off Bill, reforms to the Child Protection laws, adoption reform bills, and a bill stipulating zero tolerance for underage drinking.

Fundraising is the area she least likes about politics. On the other hand, "working with such diverse groups of people ... I enjoy working in a bi-partisan manner," is what True enjoys most.

True said her husband and staff members Barbara Kauffman and Jennifer Kennard are those who have helped her most in her career.

Since her election, True believes she has changed her way of looking at things. "Being elected to the House has been like going on to higher education. I have learned so much about so many issues. I think now on a broader level," she said.

She would like to be remembered as "someone who was

effective and someone who keeps her word."

True was named executive director of the Pennsylvania Commission for Women by Governor Tom Ridge following her unsuccessful run for the office of auditor general against Robert Casey, Jr. in November of 2000.

Varallo, Mary A. (D) Philadelphia
(resigned January 4, 1960)
1945-46 and 1949-60

Varallo, born June 12, 1897 in Philadelphia, Pa., was the daughter of Augustus and Kathryne Frascone. Varallo graduated from the Peirce School of Business, the Charles Morris Price School of Advertising and Journalism, Temple University's School of Commerce and studied political science at the University of Pennsylvania.

She was not only an accomplished composer, pianist and organist, teaching music to the children of Philadelphia, but also a professional jeweler.

Her political achievements are remarkable. Varallo was the first woman to serve as a Democratic Caucus chairman, minority and majority whips, and executive member of the Joint State Government Commission. She authored the Women's Equal Rights bill that passed and became law on May 17, 1945.

Varallo also served as the chairman of the House Welfare Committee and as vice chairman of the Banking Committee.

Varallo was the organizer and president of the Women's Democratic Club of Philadelphia, founder and president of the Italian-American Women's Democratic Club of Philadelphia, secretary and vice chairman of the Democratic City Committee and member of the Democratic State Executive Committee. She was a delegate to two Democratic National Conventions and a member of the Electoral College in 1960.

She received awards such as Distinguished Daughter of Pennsylvania, in 1959, the Italian Republic's Star of Solidarity from

174

the president of Italy, in 1958, and Outstanding Catholic Woman of the Year by the Knights of Columbus San Domingo Council.

Varallo resigned January 4, 1960, from the House so that she could assume her new elected position as Philadelphia Councilman-at-Large. She served in this position until 1968.

In 1968, while being considered as a candidate for treasurer of the United States, Varallo entered the Democratic primary for the U.S. Congress. She lost to incumbent Congressman James Byrne.

Varallo died November 27, 1979, at the age of 82.

Weston, Frances (R) Philadelphia
1981-90

Weston, who was once called a "real ball of dynamite" by one GOP leader, was born on September 1, 1954, in Philadelphia. She is the daughter of Alfred W. and Patricia Morgan Peteraf.

Weston attended St. Hubert's High School and continued her education at Temple University where she earned a bachelor's degree in political science.

Weston was a member of the American Legion Oxley Post Women's Auxiliary, Pennsylvania Polish American Citizens's League, Philadelphia Day Care Task Force and on the Frankford Hospital board.

She won her first election to the House by over 2,000 votes. Weston once accepted a New York weekend trip and stayed at a posh hotel – a gift of Bell of Pennsylvania. She was criticized after the legal gift was widely reported in the press. As a result, she declined all future gifts from lobbyists.

"We have an obligation to be careful because, whether we want to admit it or not, they do influence us in some way. We're only human," she said.

Whittlesey, Faith Ryan (R) Delaware
1973-75

Twice Ambassador to Switzerland, top staff to President Ronald Reagan and once candidate for lieutenant governor, Whittlesey also served as a Delaware County Council member and chairman and U.S. assistant attorney general.

Born on February 21, 1939, in Jersey City, N.J., Whittlesey is the daughter of Marlin R. Ryan and Amy Covell Ryan. She graduated Phi Beta Kappa from Wells College in 1960, the University of Pennsylvania Law School in 1963 and received a Ford Foundation grant during law school to attend the Academy of International Law, The Hague, in the Netherlands.

Married to Roger Weaver Whittlesey, they had three children. Their third child, in fact, was born three weeks prior to Whittlesey's election to the House.

Her husband was supportive of Whittelsey's interest in politics. "I like it very much," he said, "I really believe a marriage is enriched when women can have something outside the family to orient to. After 10 years, our marriage is as good as when it started."

Following her first election Whittlesey, a new mother, admitted that she was "very tired."

"I think," she said, "the fact that I'm a woman hurt me in some ways and helped me in some ways. I had a lot of comments that a women's place is in the home. I feel I can be a good mother and a good legislator. The two are not incompatible."

As a freshmen legislator Whittlesey was concerned with spending. Her first order of business was to suggest legislation eliminating local tax collector positions, which she thought were "totally wasteful."

In 1981 and again in 1985 Whittlesey was named Ambassador to Switzerland. In the interim, for two years she served as assistant for public liaison at the White House, the highest-ranking woman on President Reagan's staff, replacing Elizabeth Dole

176

who had been named Transportation secretary.

When appointed by Reagan in 1981, the Philadelphia Inquirer ran the following comments in an editorial: "President Reagan's designation of Faith Ryan Whittlesey as ambassador to Switzerland assures the United States of a top flight representative at one of the most valuable diplomatic watchtowers in all Europe... she has been deeply, and admirably, involved in politics, and one thing her selection for the ambassadorial post serves to point up is the relative scarcity at this time of other outstanding women in politics in Pennsylvania. It may be that Faith is showing the way to a return to the recognition and prestige which were once the hallmarks of female politicians in this state."

Wilson, Jean L. (R) Philadelphia
(elected to replace Benjamin H. Wilson, who died of a heart attack on March 6, 1988)
1989-92

Wilson was born on June 13, 1928, in Philadelphia.

Wilson won her first election by a margin of almost 6,000 votes, carrying on the tradition and name of her late husband. Two years later, she was reelected for her final term as a representative in the state House.

Wilson has a bachelor's degree from Pennsylvania State University and is a former teacher. She also was employed as an office manager and executive secretary.

She was a member of many organizations, including the Bucks County Council of Republican Women, Warminster Republican Club, Pennridge Republican Club, North Penn Council of Republican Women and Chi Omega Alumni Association.

Wilson has two daughters.

Wilson, Lilith M. (Socialist) Berks
1931-36

The first woman to run for governor in Pennsylvania, Lilith Martin Wilson led not only the Socialist Party into the political fray but also paved the way for women in the legislature as the first Socialist woman to be elected to any legislative body in the United States.

Born in Wayne County, Indiana, she moved to Reading in the early 1920s where she married L. Birch Wilson, a local official, and settled into the life of an active participant in the Socialist Party.

She graduated from the party's Rand School of Social Science and lectured throughout the country as well as organized events and campaigns for the party. In 1921, she was elected to the National Executive Committee of the Socialist Party, and it was then that she moved to Pennsylvania to help mobilize campaigns in Reading and the state.

It was in 1922 that the party nominated Wilson as their candidate for Pennsylvania's governor. After she lost the election, she ran for the Reading School Board in 1923.

The Socialist Party then became to come into its own in the Reading area, and by 1927, the party gained control over the city government and maintained this control for the next 8 years. It was during this time, in 1928, that Wilson ran for state treasurer.

She was the first woman elected from Berks County.

Wilson was involved in many local and national organizations including as a member of the League for Industrial Democracy, the Old Age Security League and the Board of Directors of the Birth Control League of Berks County.

Winter, Elizabeth A. (R) Philadelphia
1963-64

Winter was born in Philadelphia on March 3, 1928, the daughter of Walter I. and Anna C. Anderson Watson. She attended Lowell School and Olney High School.

Her political career began when she ran for a Republican committeewoman slot, and won, leading the 38th Division, 23rd Ward for eight years in the late fifties.

She was the chairman of the 23rd Ward Republican Executive Committee.

Winter's memberships in clubs include the Women's Republican Club of the 23rd Ward, the Philadelphia Congress of Republican Councils, and the Sullivan Home and School Association.

Winter was a former secretary and office manager to a dean at the University of Pennsylvania. She also was employed by the Philadelphia Municipal Court where she was a supervisor of court reporters for 27 years.

Winter died on September 21, 1993.

Wise, D.Ed. Helen Dickerson (D) Centre)
1977-78

"Cares, communicates and serves people," was Wise's campaign-winning slogan, which allowed her a sweeping victory over her 1976 opponent for the House.

Her leadership and her concern for her fellow representatives from her neighboring districts to "work as a team to help the constituents," ensured her success in the House.

The lawmaker's special interests were in education and agriculture.

She was born on September 11, 1928, in Sussex, New Jersey and is the daughter of Russell B. and Josephine C. Miles Dickerson.

179

Growing up in Centre County, Wise graduated from State College High School and continued her education at Pennsylvania State University. At Penn State, she earned bachelor, masters and doctoral degrees.

As a public school teacher at a State College junior high school, Wise served as the president of both the Pennsylvania State Education Association and the National Education Association.

Teaching was only one of her careers. Wife, mother and grandmother of three, she also is an accomplished author who wrote books and articles on education and American society.

Her book, <u>What Do We Tell the Children? Watergate and the Future of Our Country</u>, addressed her concerns for the future of American society.

Wise served as Governor Robert P.Casey's Legislative Secretary, his liaison to the cabinet, and as one of his senior advisors.

While working in Casey administration, Wise directed the highly successful "Capital for a Day" Program whereby all the top officials in state government, including the governor and lieutenant governor and cabinet members, traveled to several communities to conduct the state's business.

Wynd, Elizabeth S. [Wallace]* (R) Wyoming
(elected May 16, 1961 vice James Wynd, Jr., who died)
*Married Frank R. Wallace in 1965.
1961-66

Wynd, born February 16, 1914, in Tunkhannock, served after winning a special election.

Replacing her deceased husband, James Wynd, Jr., who died while serving as a Representative of Wyoming County, Wynd filled his seat for the remainder of his term, then campaigned and won two subsequent terms.

Wynd graduated from Wyoming Seminary and the Dean

180

School of Business where she became a law secretary. She also worked as a county reporter. She also served as a Wyoming deputy county treasurer and chairman of the Legislative Committee of Wyoming County Republicans.

Her first husband, in addition to his service in the House, was the sheriff of Wyoming County. In 1965, Wynd married Frank R. Wallace, secretary treasurer of the Pennsylvania Gas and Water Company.

Wynd died January 25, 1974.

APPENDICES

APPENDICES

Appendix I

The 101 Women of the Pennsylvania House of Representatives 1923-2001

Alphabetical List

Name, Affiliation, County	Dates Served
Adams, Ella Collier (R) Fayette	1927-30
Alexander, Jane M. (D) York	1965-68
Anderson, Sarah A. (D) Philadelphia	1955-72
Arty, Mary Ann [Majors] (R) Delaware	1979-88
Baker, Jane S. (R) Lehigh	2001-
Bard, Ellen M. (R) Montgomery	1995-
Bebko-Jones, Linda (D) Erie	1993-
Bentley, Alice M. (R) Crawford	1923-28*
Bishop, Louise Williams (D) Philadelphia	1989-
Boscola, Lisa M. (D) Northampton	1995-98
Brancato, Anna M. [Wood]	

(D) Philadelphia	1933-40 & 1945-46
Brugger, Jeanne D. (R) Montgomery	1965-66
Burns, Barbara A. (D) Allegheny	
(elected March 7, 1994 vice	
Thomas Murphy who resigned)	1994
Carone, Patricia Ann [Krebs]	
(D/R) Butler	1991-98
Clark, Rita (R) Cambria	1979-80
Cohen, Lita Indzel (R) Montgomery	1993-
Coyle, Josephine C. (D) Philadelphia	1945-46 & 1951-54
Crawford, Evelyn Glazier Henzel (R)	
Montgomery	1955-62
Crawford, Patricia A. (R) Chester	1969-76
Dailey, Mary Ann (R) Montgomery	1999-
Denman, Mary Thompson (R)	
Westmoreland	1931-32
de Young, Rosa Stein (R) Philadelphia	1923-24*
Donahue, Ruth Stover (R)	
Clinton	1955-60
Duffy, Mary Alice (D) Philadelphia	1957-58
Durham, Kathrynann Walrath (R)	
Delaware	1979-96
Dye, Jeanette M. (R) Mercer	1945-50
Farmer, Elaine F. (R) Allegheny	1987-96
Fauset, Crystal Bird (D) Philadelphia	1939-40
1st African-Amer	
Fawcett, Charlotte D. (R) Montgomery	1971-76
Forcier, Teresa E. Brown (R) Crawford	1991-
Gallagher Ph.D., Sarah McCune (R)	
Cambria	1923-24*
George, Lourene Walker (R)	

Cumberland	1963-70
George, Margaret H. (D) Bucks	1977-80
Gillette, Helen D. (D) Allegheny	1967-78
Grimes, Helen (R) Allegheny	1923-30*
Hagarty, Lois Sherman (R)	
Montgomery *(elected in special*	
election March 11, 1980)	1980-92
Harhart, Julie (R) Northampton	1995-
Harley, Ellen A. (R) Montgomery	1991-94
Harper, Catherine M. "Kate" (R)	
Montgomery	2001-
Harper, Ruth B. (D) Philadelphia	1977-92
Heiser, Loraine [Lori] (R) Allegheny	1981-82
Honaman, June N. (R) Lancaster	1977-88
Horting, Ruth Grigg (D) Lancaster	1937-38
Jones, Frances R. (D) Philadelphia	
(elected May 19, 1959	
vice Granville Jones, who died)	1959-66
Josephs, Babette (D) Philadelphia	1985-
Kelly, Anita Palermo (D) Philadelphia	
(elected Nov. 5, 1963	
vice William J. Kelly,	
her husband, who died)	1963-78
Kernaghan, Mae Winter (R) Delaware	1957-70
Kernick, Phyllis T. (D) Allegheny	1975-80
Kirkbride, Mabelle M. (R) Montgomery	1929-32
Kitchen, Shirley M. (D) Philadelphia	
(special election, vice	
Alphonso Deal, who died	
June 3, 1987)	1987-88
Kooker, Margarette S. (R) Bucks	1955-66

Langtry, Alice S. (R) Allegheny 1985-92
Laughlin, Susan (D) Beaver 1989-
Lederer, Marie A. (D) Philadelphia 1993-
Leiby, Mary E. (D) Lehigh 1955-56
Lewis, Marilyn Stoughton (R)
    Montgomery 1979-82

Mackereth, Beverly L. (R) York 2001-
MacKinney, Sarah Gertrude (R) Butler 1923-24*
Maine, Constance "Connie" G. (D)
    Crawford 1987-90
Major, Sandra J. (R) Susquehanna 1995-
Manderino, Kathy M. (D) Philadelphia 1993-
Mann, Jennifer L. (D) Lehigh 1999-
Markley, Marian E. (R) Lehigh 1951-68
McCosker, Henrietta C. (R) Philadelphia 1947-48
McHale, Katherine Pecka (D) Lehigh 1991-92
McHugh, Connie Black (R) Philadelphia 1991-92
Miller, Beatrice Z. (R) Philadelphia 1957-60
Miller, Sheila M. (R) Berks 1993-
Monroe, Susie (D) Philadelphia 1949-68
Mundy, Phyllis Block (D) Luzerne 1991-
Munley, Marion L. (D) Lackawanna
    (replaced her husband Robert
    W. Munley, who died, in a special
    election on Sept. 9, 1947) 1947-64

Odorisio, Helen R. (R) Delaware
    (replaced her husband, Rocco A.
    Odorisio in special election held
    July 25, 1967) 1967-68
Orie, Jane Clare (R) Allegheny 1997-

Pashley, Kathryn Graham (D) 1955-66
    Philadelphia

Pennock, Martha M. (R) Philadelphia 1925-34
Pickett, Tina L. (R)
Pitts, Lillie H. (R) Philadelphia 1923-32*

Reibman, Jeanette F. (D) Northampton 1955-56 & 1959-66
Ritter, Karen A. (D) Lehigh 1987-94
Rubley, Carole A. (R) Chester 1993-
Rudy, Ruth Corman (D) Centre 1983-96

Scanlon, Agnes Ruddock (D) 1977-78
    Philadelphia
Seyfert, Ph.D., R. Tracy (R) Crawford 1997-2000
Sheehan, Ph.D., Colleen A. (R)
    Montgomery 1995-96
Sirianni, Carmel A. (R) Susquehanna 1975-88
Speiser, Martha G. (R) Philadelphia 1923-24*
Steelman, Ph.D., Sara Gerling (D)
    Indiana 1991-

Taylor, Elinor Gene Zimmerman (R)
    Chester 1977-
Telek, Leona G. (R) Cambria 1989-92
Thomas, Martha G. (R) Chester 1923-26*
Toll, Rose (D) Philadelphia 1971-76
Trescher, Maud Byers (R) 1925-26
    Westmoreland
True, Katie Buck (R) Lancaster 1993-2000

Vance, Patricia Huston (R) Cumberland 1991-
Varallo, Mary A. (D) Philadelphia
    (resigned Jan.4, 1960) 1945-46 & 1949-60

Washington, LeAnna M. (D) Philadelphia
    (elected Nov. 2, 1993 vice Gordon
    Linton, who resigned) 1993-

188

Watson, Katherine M. (R) Bucks	2001-
Weston, Frances (R) Philadelphia	1981-90
Whittlesey, Faith Ryan (R) Delaware	1973-75
Williams, Constance H. "Connie" (D) Montgomery	1997-
Wilson, Jean T. (R) Philadelphia	1989-92
Wilson, Lilith M. (Socialist) Berks	1931-36
Winter, Elizabeth A. (R) Philadelphia	1963-64
Wise, D.Ed. Helen Dickerson (D) Centre	1977-78
Wynd, Elizabeth S. (R) Wyoming *(elected May 16, 1961 vice James Wynd, Jr.,her husband, who died)*	1961-66
Youngblood, Rosita C. (D) Philadelphia *(elected Apr. 5, 1994 vice Robert O'Donnell who resigned)*	1994-

*One of the original eight women first elected to the House for the 1923-24 session.

Appendix II

Women in the House
Chronological House Session

1923-24 *Sworn in on Tuesday, January 2, 1923*

	Occupation
Bentley, Alice M. (R-Crawford)	teacher
deYoung, Rosa Stein (R-Philadelphia)	housewife, community volunteer
Gallagher, Ph.D. Sarah McCune (R-Cambria)	teacher
Grimes, Helen (R-Allegheny)	
MacKinney, Sarah Gertrude (R-Butler)	librarian
Pitts, Lillie H. (R-Philadelphia)	
Speiser, Martha G. (R-Philadelphia)	
Thomas, Martha G. (R-Chester)	

1925-26

Bentley, Alice M. (R-Crawford)	insurance
Grimes, Helen (R-Allegheny)	housekeeper
Pennock, Martha M. (R-Philadelphia)	housewife
Pitts, Lillie H. (R-Philadelphia)	housewife
Thomas, Martha G. (R-Chester)	farmer
Trescher, Maud Byers (R-Westmoreland)	housewife

1927-28

Adams, Ella Collier (R-Fayette)	housewife
Bentley, Alice M. (R-Crawford)	insurance
Grimes, Helen (R-Allegheny)	housekeeper
Pennock, Martha M. (R-Philadelphia)	
Pitts, Lillie H. (R-Philadelphia)	housewife

1929-30

Adams, Ella Collier (R-Fayette)	housewife
Grimes, Helen (R-Allegheny)	housekeeper
Kirkbride, Mabelle M. (R-Montgomery)	teacher, housewife
Pennock, Martha M. (R-Philadephia)	
Pitts, Lillie H. (R-Philadelphia)	housewife

1931-32

Denman, Mary T. (R-Westmoreland)	attorney
Kirkbride, Mabelle M. (R-Montgomery)	housewife
Pennock, Martha M. (R-Philadephia)	
Pitts, Lillie H. (R-Philadelphia)	housewife
Wilson, Lilith M. (Socialist-Berks)	lecturer

1933-34

Brancato, Anna M. [Wood] (D-Philadelphia)	real estate and insurance broker
Pennock, Martha M. (R-Philadephia)	
Wilson, Lilith M. (Socialist-Berks)	lecturer

1935-36

Brancato, Anna M.[Wood] (D-Philadelphia)	real estate and insurance broker
Wilson, Lilith M. (Socialist-Berks)	lecturer

1937-38

Brancato, Anna M. [Wood] (D-Philadelphia)	real estate and insurance broker
Horting, Ruth Grigg (D-Lancaster)	housewife

1939-40

Brancato, Anna M. [Wood] (D-Philadelphia)	real estate and insurance broker

191

Fauset, Crystal Bird (D-Philadelphia)   civic worker

1941-42 NO WOMEN SERVED IN THIS SESSION

1943-44 NO WOMEN SERVED IN THIS SESSION

1945-46
Brancato, Anna M.[Wood]
    (D-Philadelphia)   real estate and
                                    insurance broker
Coyle, Josephine C. (D-Philadelphia)   housewife
Dye, Jeanette M. (R-Mercer)   housewife
Varallo, Mary A. (D-Philadelphia)   jeweler

1947-48
Dye, Jeanette M. (R-Mercer)   housewife
McCosker, Henrietta C. (R-Philadelphia) municipal court
                                    supervisor
Munley, Marion L. (D-Lackawanna)   housewife,
                                    community volunteer,
                                    labor activist

1949-50
Dye, Jeanette M. (R-Mercer)   housewife
Monroe, Susie (D-Philadelphia)   dressmaker
Munley, Marion L. (D-Lackawanna)   housewife,
                                    community volunteer,
                                    labor activist
Varallo, Mary A. (D-Philadelphia)   jeweler

1951-52
Coyle, Josephine C. (D-Philadelphia)   housewife
Markley, Marian E. (R-Lehigh)   office manager,
                                    secretary
Monroe, Susie (D-Philadelphia)   dressmaker
Munley, Marion L. (D-Lackawanna)   housewife,
                                    community volunteer,
                                    labor activist

192

Varallo, Mary A. (D-Philadelphia)   jeweler

1953-54
Coyle, Josephine C. (D-Philadelphia)   housewife
Markley, Marian E. (R-Lehigh)   office manager,
                                           secretary
Monroe, Susie (D-Philadelphia)   dressmaker
Munley, Marion L. (D-Lackawanna)   housewife,
                                           community volunteer,
                                           labor activist
Varallo, Mary A. (D-Philadelphia)   jeweler

1955-56
Anderson, Sarah A. (D-Philadelphia)   teacher
Crawford, Evelyn Glazier [Henzel]
    (R-Montgomery)   teacher, housewife
Donahue, Ruth Stover (R-Clinton)   teacher
Kooker, Margarette S. (R-Bucks)   furniture business
Leiby, Mary E. (D-Lehigh)   teacher
Markley, Marian E. (R-Lehigh)   office manager,
                                           secretary
Monroe, Susie (D-Philadelphia)   dressmaker
Munley, Marion L. (D-Lackawanna)   housewife,
                                           community volunteer,
                                           labor activist
Pashley, Kathryn Graham
    (D-Philadelphia)   community volunteer,
                                           housewife
Reibman, Jeanette F. (D-Northampton)   attorney
Varallo, Mary A. (D-Philadelphia)   jeweler

1957-58
Anderson, Sarah A. (D-Philadelphia)   teacher
Crawford, Evelyn Glazier [Henzel]
    (R-Montgomery)   teacher, housewife
Donahue, Ruth Stover (R-Clinton)   teacher
Duffy, Mary Alice (D-Philadelphia)   attorney

193

Kernaghan, Mae Winter (R-Delaware)	community volunteer
Kooker, Margarette S. (R-Bucks)	furniture business
Markley, Marian E. (R-Lehigh)	office manager, secretary
Miller, Beatrice Z. (R-Philadelphia)	community volunteer, political activist
Monroe, Susie (D-Philadelphia)	dressmaker
Munley, Marion L. (D-Lackawanna)	housewife, community volunteer, labor activist
Pashley, Kathryn Graham (D-Philadelphia)	community volunteer, housewife
Varallo, Mary A. (D-Philadelphia)	jeweler

1959-60

Anderson, Sarah A. (D-Philadelphia)	teacher
Crawford, Evelyn Glazier [Henzel] (R-Montgomery)	teacher, housewife
Donahue, Ruth Stover (R-Clinton)	teacher
Jones, Frances R. (D-Philadelphia)	housewife
Kernaghan, Mae Winter (R-Delaware)	community volunteer
Kooker, Margarette S. (R-Bucks)	furniture business
Markley, Marian E. (R-Lehigh)	office manager, secretary
Miller, Beatrice Z. (R-Philadelphia)	community volunteer, political activist
Monroe, Susie (D-Philadelphia)	dressmaker
Munley, Marion L. (D-Lackawanna)	housewife, community volunteer, labor activist
Pashley, Kathryn Graham (D-Philadelphia)	community volunteer, housewife
Reibman, Jeanette F. (D-Northampton)	attorney
Varallo, Mary A. (D-Philadelphia)	jeweler

194

1961-62

Anderson, Sarah A. (D-Philadelphia)	teacher
Crawford, Evelyn Glazier [Henzel] (R-Montgomery)	teacher, housewife
Jones, Frances R. (D-Philadelphia)	housewife
Kernaghan, Mae Winter (R-Delaware)	community volunteer
Kooker, Margarette S. (R-Bucks)	furniture business
Markley, Marian E. (R-Lehigh)	office manager, secretary
Monroe, Susie (D-Philadelphia)	dressmaker
Munley, Marion L. (D-Lackawanna)	housewife, community volunteer, labor activist
Pashley, Kathryn Graham (D-Philadelphia)	community volunteer, housewife
Reibman, Jeanette F. (D-Northampton)	attorney
Wynd, Elizabeth Steele (R-Wyoming)	housewife, county treasurer, secretary

1963-64

Anderson, Sarah A. (D-Philadelphia)	teacher, housewife
George, Lourene Walker (R-Cumberland)	nurse-anesthetist
Jones, Frances R. (D-Philadelphia)	housewife
Kelly, Anita Palermo (D-Philadelphia)	
Kernaghan, Mae Winter (R-Delaware)	community volunteer
Kooker, Margarette S. (R-Bucks)	furniture business
Markley, Marian E. (R-Lehigh)	office manager, secretary, admin. assist.
Monroe, Susie (D-Philadelphia)	dressmaker
Munley, Marion L. (D-Lackawanna)	housewife, community volunteer, labor activist

195

Pashley, Kathryn Graham
    (D-Philadelphia)   community volunteer,
                                      housewife
Reibman, Jeanette F. (D-Northampton)   attorney
Winter, Elizabeth A. (R-Philadelphia)   housewife,
                                      university dean's
                                      secy
Wynd, Elizabeth Steele (R-Wyoming)   housewife,
                                      county treasurer,
                                      secretary

1965-66

Alexander, Jane M. (D-York)   attorney
Anderson, Sarah A. (D-Philadelphia)   teacher, housewife
Brugger, Jeanne D. (R-Montgomery)   psychologist,
                                      college teacher
George, Lourene Walker (R-Cumberland) nurse anesthetist
Jones, Frances R. (D-Philadelphia)
Kelly, Anita Palermo (D-Philadelphia)
Kernaghan, Mae Winter (R-Delaware)   community
                                      volunteer
Kooker, Margarette S. (R-Bucks)   furniture business
Markley, Marian E. (R-Lehigh)   office manager,
                                      secretary
Monroe, Susie (D-Philadelphia)   dressmaker
Pashley, Kathryn Graham
    (D-Philadelphia)   community volunteer,
                                      housewife
Reibman, Jeanette F. (D-Northampton)   attorney
Wynd, Elizabeth Steele (R-Wyoming)   housewife,
                                      county treasurer,
                                      secretary

1967-68

Alexander, Jane M. (D-York)   attorney
Anderson, Sarah A. (D-Philadelphia)   teacher, housewife
George, Lourene Walker (R-Cumberland) nurse anesthetist

Gillette, Helen D. (D-Allegheny)   insurance agent
                                            and accountant
Kelly, Anita Palermo (D-Philadelphia)
Kernaghan, Mae Winter (R-Delaware)   community
                                            volunteer
Markley, Marian E. (R-Lehigh)   office manager,
                                            secretary
Monroe, Susie (D-Philadelphia)   dressmaker
Odorisio, Helen R. (R-Delaware)   nurse

1969-70
Anderson, Sarah A. (D-Philadelphia)   teacher, housewife
Crawford, Patricia A. (R-Chester)   homemaker,
                                            community
                                            volunteer
George, Lourene Walker (R-Cumberland) nurse anesthetist
Gillette, Helen D. (D-Allegheny)   insurance agent
                                            and accountant
Kelly, Anita Palermo (D-Philadelphia)
Kernaghan, Mae Winter (R-Delaware)   community
                                            volunteer
1971-72
Anderson, Sarah A. (D-Philadelphia)   teacher, housewife
Crawford, Patricia A. (R-Chester)   homemaker,
                                            community volunteer
Fawcett, Charlotte D. (R-Bucks, Montgomery)
Gillette, Helen D. (D-Allegheny)   insurance agent
                                            and accountant
Kelly, Anita Palermo (D-Philadelphia)
Toll, Rose Ornstein (D-Philadelphia)   registered nurse

1973-74
Crawford, Patricia A. (R-Chester)   homemaker,
                                            community volunteer
Fawcett, Charlotte D. (R-Bucks, Montgomery)
Gillette, Helen D. (D-Allegheny)   insurance agent
                                            and accountant

197

Kelly, Anita Palermo (D-Philadelphia)

Toll, Rose Ornstein (D-Philadelphia)   registered nurse

1973-74
Crawford, Patricia A. (R-Chester)   homemaker,
                                           community
                                           volunteer
Fawcett, Charlotte D. (R-Bucks, Montgomery)
Gillette, Helen D. (D-Allegheny)   insurance agent
                                           and accountant
Kelly, Anita Palermo (D-Philadelphia)
Toll, Rose Ornstein (D-Philadelphia)   registered nurse
Whittlesey, Faith Ryan (R-Delaware)   attorney

1975-76
Crawford, Patricia A. (R-Chester)   homemaker,
                                           community
                                           volunteer
Fawcett, Charlotte D. (R-Bucks, Montgomery)
Gillette, Helen D. (D-Allegheny)   insurance agent
                                           and accountant
Kelly, Anita Palermo (D-Philadelphia)
Kernick, Phyllis T. (D-Allegheny)   township
                                           treasurer
Sirianni, Carmel A. (R-Bradford, Susquehanna,
          Sullivan, Wyoming Counties)   teacher
Toll, Rose Ornstein (D-Philadelphia)   registered nurse
Whittlesey, Faith Ryan (R-Delaware)   attorney
          (resigned 12/31/75)

1977-78
George, Margaret "Peg" H. (D-Bucks)   housewife
Gillette, Helen D. (D-Allegheny)   insurance agent
                                           and accountant
Harper, Ruth B. (D-Philadelphia)   charm/modeling
                                           school director

198

Honaman, June N. (R-Lancaster)   housewife
Kelly, Anita Palermo (D-Philadelphia)
Kernick, Phyllis T. (D-Allegheny)
Scanlon, Agnes M. Ruddock
        (D-Philadelphia)   beautician
Sirianni, Carmel A. (R-Bradford, Susquehanna,
        Sullivan, Wyoming Counties)   teacher
Taylor, Elinor Gene Zimmerman
        (R-Chester)   college professor
Wise, D.Ed. Helen Dickerson (D-Centre) teacher, author

1979-80

Arty, Mary Ann [Majors] (R-Delaware)   registered nurse
Clark, Rita (R-Cambria)   teacher
Durham, Kathrynann Walrath
        (R-Delaware)   attorney, teacher
George, Margaret "Peg" H. (D-Bucks)   housewife
Hagarty, Lois Sherman (R-Montgomery)   attorney
Harper, Ruth B. (D-Philadelphia)   charm/modeling
                                       school director
Honaman, June N. (R-Lancaster)   housewife
Kernick, Phyllis T. (D-Allegheny)
Lewis, Marilyn Stoughton
        (R-Montgomery)   housewife,
                                       licensed pilot
Sirianni, Carmel A. (R-Bradford, Susquehanna,
        Sullivan, Wyoming Counties)   teacher
Taylor, Elinor Gene Zimmerman
        (R-Chester)   college professor

1981-82

Arty, Mary Ann [Majors] (R-Delaware)   registered nurse
Durham, Kathrynann Walrath
        (R-Delaware)   attorney, teacher
Harper, Ruth B. (D-Philadelphia)   charm/modeling
                                       school director
Hagarty, Lois Sherman (R-Montgomery)   attorney

199

Heiser, Loraine "Lori" (R-Allegheny)   home economist,
                                           dietitian,teacher
Honaman, June N. (R-Lancaster)   housewife
Lewis, Marilyn Stoughton
    (R-Montgomery)   housewife,
                                           licensed pilot
Sirianni, Carmel A. (R-Bradford, Susquehanna,
    Sullivan, Wyoming Counties)   teacher
Taylor, Elinor Gene Zimmerman
    (R-Chester)   college professor
Weston, Frances "Fran" Peteraf
    (R-Philadelphia)   accounting supervisor

1983-84

Arty, Mary Ann [Majors] (R-Delaware) registered nurse
Durham, Kathrynann Walrath
    (R-Delaware)   attorney, teacher
Hagarty, Lois Sherman (R-Montgomery) attorney
Harper, Ruth B. (D-Philadelphia)   charm/modeling
                                           school director
Honaman, June N. (R-Lancaster)   housewife
Rudy, Ruth Corman (D-Centre,Mifflin) prothonotary
Sirianni, Carmel A. (R-Bradford, Susquehanna,
    Sullivan, Wyoming Counties)   teacher
Taylor, Elinor Gene Zimmerman
    (R-Chester)   college professor
Weston, Frances "Fran" Peteraf
    (R-Philadelphia)   accounting supervisor

1985-86

Arty, Mary Ann [Majors] (R-Delaware) registered nurse
Durham, Kathrynann Walrath
    (R-Delaware)   attorney, teacher
Hagarty, Lois Sherman
    (R-Montgomery)   attorney
Harper, Ruth B. (D-Philadelphia)   charm/modeling
                                           school director
Honaman, June N. (R-Lancaster)   housewife

200

Josephs, Babette (D-Philadelphia)	attorney
Langtry, Alice S. (R-Allegheny)	corporate administration
Rudy, Ruth Corman (D-Centre,Mifflin)	prothonotary
Sirianni, Carmel A. (R-Bradford, Susquehanna, Sullivan, Wyoming Counties)	teacher
Taylor, Elinor Gene Zimmerman (R-Chester)	college professor
Weston, Frances "Fran" Peteraf (R-Philadelphia)	accounting supervisor

1987-88

Arty, Mary Ann [Majors] (R-Delaware)	registered nurse
Durham, Kathrynann Walrath (R-Delaware)	attorney, teacher
Farmer, Elaine F. (R-Allegheny)	teacher, businesswoman
Hagarty, Lois Sherman (R-Montgomery)	attorney
Harper, Ruth B. (D-Philadelphia)	charm/modeling school director
Honaman, June N. (R-Lancaster)	housewife
Josephs, Babette (D-Philadelphia)	attorney
Kitchen, Shirley M. (D-Philadelphia)	social work
Langtry, Alice S. (R-Allegheny)	corporate administration
Maine, Constance "Connie" G. (D-Crawford)	consultant, counselor, lecturer
Ritter, Karen A. (D-Lehigh)	paralegal, title insurance manager
Rudy, Ruth Corman (D-Centre, Mifflin)	prothonotary
Sirianni, Carmel A. (R-Bradford, Susquehanna, Sullivan, Wyoming)	teacher
Taylor, Elinor Gene Zimmerman (R-Chester)	college professor
Weston, Frances "Fran" Peterof (R-Philadelphia)	

1989-90

Bishop, Louise Williams (D-Philadelphia) Baptist Evangelist minister

Durham, Kathrynann Walrath
   (R-Delaware) attorney, teacher

Farmer, Elaine F. (R-Allegheny) teacher, businesswoman

Hagarty, Lois Sherman (R-Montgomery) attorney

Harper, Ruth B. (D-Philadelphia) charm/modeling school director

Josephs, Babette (D-Philadelphia) attorney

Langtry, Alice S. (R-Allegheny) corporate administration

Laughlin, Susan (D-Allegheny, Beaver) community volunteer

Maine, Constance "Connie" G.
   (D-Crawford) consultant, counselor, lecturer

Mundy, Phyllis Block (D-Luzerne) business manager

Ritter, Karen A. (D-Lehigh) paralegal, title insurance manager

Rubley, Carole A. Drumm (R-Chester) environmental consultant

Rudy, Ruth Corman (D-Centre, Mifflin) prothonotary

Steelman, Ph.D Sara Gerling Ph.D.
   (D-Indiana) college psych researcher/teacher

Taylor, Elinor Gene Zimmerman
   (R-Chester) college professor

True, Katie Buck (R-Lancaster) substance abuse writer, TELLS tutor

Vance, Patricia Huston (R-Cumberland) registered nurse

Washngton, LeAnna M. (D-Philadelphia) human services

Youngblood, Rosita (D-Philadelphia) constituent serv. rep., credit adm.

1991-92

Bishop, Louise Williams
(D-Philadelphia)   Baptist Evangelist
                                                  minister

Carone, Patricia Ann[Krebs]
    (D/R-Butler, Lawrence)   educator
Durham, Kathrynann Walrath
    (R-Delaware)   attorney, teacher

Farmer, Elaine F. (R-Allegheny)   teacher, businesswoman
Forcier, Theresa E. Brown
    (R-Crawford)   asst. dir. cnty.
                                                  tax claim bureau
Hagarty, Lois Sherman
    (R-Montgomery)   attorney

Harley, Ellen A. (R-Montgomery)   city/regional planner
Harper, Ruth B. (D-Philadelphia)   charm/modeling
                                                  school director
Josephs, Babette (D-Philadelphia)   attorney
Langtry, Alice S. (R-Allegheny)   corporate administration
Laughlin, Susan (D-Allegheny,Beaver)   community volunteer
McHale, Katherine Pecka (D-Lehigh)   public relations
                                                  specialist
McHugh, Connie Black (R-Philadelphia)   court officer
Mundy, Phyllis Block (D-Luzerne)   business manager
Ritter, Karen A. (D-Lehigh)   paralegal, title
                                                  insurance manager
Rudy, Ruth Corman (D-Centre, Mifflin)   prothonotary
Steelman, Ph.D. Sara Gerling
    (D-Indiana)   college psych
                                                  researcher/teacher
Taylor, Elinor Gene Zimmerman
    (R-Chester)   college professor
Telek, Leona G. (R-Cambria, Somerset)   retail manager
Vance, Patricia Huston (R-Cumberland)   registered nurse
Wilson, Jean T. (R-Bucks)   teacher, office manager

203

1993-94

Bebko-Jones, Linda (D-Erie) Senate admin. asst., case worker

Bishop, Louise Williams (D-Philadelphia) Baptist Evangelist minister

Burns, Barbara A. (D-Allegheny)
served only 1994 legislative assistant

Carone, Patricia Ann [Krebs]
(R-Butler, Lawrence) educator

Cohen, Lita Indzel (R-Montgomery) attorney, businesswoman

Durham, Kathrynann Walrath
(R-Delaware) attorney, teacher

Farmer, Elaine F. (R-Allegheny) teacher, businesswoman

Forcier, Teresa E. Brown (R-Crawford) asst. dir. cnty. tax claim bureau

Harley, Ellen A. (R-Montgomery) city/regional planner

Josephs, Babette (D-Philadelphia) attorney

Laughlin, Susan (D-Allegheny,Beaver) community volunteer

Lederer, Marie A. (D-Philadelphia) college teacher, gov't manager

Mandarino, Kathy M. (D-Philadelphia) attorney

Miller, Sheila M. (R-Berks) newspaper editor, conservationist

Mundy, Phyllis Block (D-Luzerne) business manager

Ritter, Karen A. (D-Lehigh) paralegal, title insurance manager

Rubley, Carole A. Drumm (R-Chester) environmental consultant

Rudy, Ruth Corman (D-Centre, Mifflin) prothonotary

Steelman, Ph.D Sara Gerling Ph.D.
(D-Indiana) college psych researcher/teacher

Taylor, Elinor Gene Zimmerman
(R-Chester) college professor

True, Katie Buck (R-Lancaster) substance abuse writer, TELLS tutor

Vance, Patricia Huston (R-Cumberland) registered nurse
Youngblood, Rosita (D-Philadelphia)   constituent serv. rep.,
                                      credit adm.

1995-96

Bard, Ellen M. (R-Montgomery)   business owner,
                                      twnshp. com.
Bebko-Jones, Linda (D-Erie)   Senate admin. asst.,
                                      case worker
Bishop, Louise Williams (D-Philadelphia) Baptist Evangelist
                                      minister
Boscola, Lisa M. (D-Lehigh, Northampton) court admin.,
                                      reg. dir. PA cty.man
Carone, Patricia Ann [Krebs]
    (R-Butler, Lawrence)   educator
Cohen, Lita Indzel (R-Montgomery)   attorney,
                                      businesswoman
Durham, Kathrynann Walrath
    (R-Delaware)   attorney, teacher
Farmer, Elaine F. (R-Allegheny)   teacher,
                                      businesswoman
Forcier, Teresa E. Brown (R-Crawford) asst. dir. cnty.
                                      tax claim bureau
Harhart, Julie (R-Lehigh, Northampton) legislative aide
Josephs, Babette (D-Philadelphia)   attorney
Laughlin, Susan (D-Allegheny,Beaver) community volunteer
Lederer, Marie A. (D-Philadelphia)   college teacher,
                                      gov't manager
Major, Sandra J. (R-Sullivan,
    Susquehanna, Wyoming)   former county
                                      treasurer
Manderino, Kathy M. (D-Philadelphia) attorney
Miller, Sheila M. (R-Berks)   newspaper editor,
                                      conservationist
Mundy, Phyllis Block (D-Luzerne)   business manager
Rubley, Carole A. Drumm (R-Chester)   environmental
                                      consultant
Rudy, Ruth Corman (D-Centre, Mifflin) prothonotary

205

Sheehan, Ph.D. Colleen A.
(R-Montgomery)   college professor

Steelman, Ph.D. Sara Gerling
(D-Indiana)   college psych
                                        researcher/teacher
Taylor, Elinor Gene Zimmerman
(R-Chester)   college professor
True, Katie Buck (R-Lancaster)   substance abuse
                                        writer, TELLS tutor
Vance, Patricia Huston (R-Cumberland)   registered nurse
Washington, LeAnna M. (D-Philadelphia) human services
Youngblood, Rosita C. (D-Philadelphia) constituent serv. rep.,
                                        credit adm.

1997-98
Bard, Ellen M. (R-Montgomery)   business owner,
twnshp. com. 153rd
Bebko-Jones, Linda (D-Erie)   Senate admin. asst.,
                                        case worker
Bishop, Louise Williams (D-Philadelphia) Baptist Evangelist
                                        minister
Boscola, Lisa M. (D-Lehigh, Northampton)   court admin.,
                                        reg. dir. PA cty.man
Carone, Patricia Ann [Krebs]
(R-Butler, Lawrence)   educator
Cohen, Lita Indzel (R-Montgomery)   attorney,
                                        businesswoman
Forcier, Teresa E. Brown (R-Crawford)   asst. dir. cnty.
                                        tax claim bureau
Harhart, Julie (R-Lehigh, Northampton) legislative aide
Josephs, Babette (D-Philadelphia)   attorney
Laughlin, Susan (D-Allegheny,Beaver)   community
                                        volunteer
Lederer, Marie A. (D-Philadelphia)   college teacher,
                                        gov't manager
Major, Sandra J. (R-Sullivan, Susquehanna,
Wyoming)   former county
                                        treasurer

206

Manderino, Kathy M. (D-Philadelphia)	attorney
Miller, Sheila M. (R-Berks)	newspaper editor, conservationist
Mundy, Phyllis Block (D-Luzerne)	business manager
Orie, Jane Clare (R-Allegheny)	attorney
Rubley, Carole A. Drumm (R-Chester)	environmental consultant
Seyfert, Ph.D. R. Tracy (R-Erie, Crawford)	psychologist
Steelman, Ph.D. Sara Gerling (D-Indiana)	college psych researcher/teacher
Taylor, Elinor Gene Zimmerman (R-Chester)	college professor
True, Katie Buck (R-Lancaster)	substance abuse writer, TELLS tutor
Vance, Patricia Huston (R-Cumberland)	registered nurse
Washington, LeAnna M. (D-Philadelphia)	human services
Williams, Constance "Connie" Hess (D-Montgomery)	congressional aide
Youngblood, Rosita C. (D-Philadelphia)	constituent serv. rep., credit adm.

1999-2000

Bard, Ellen M. (R-Montgomery)	business owner, twnshp. com.
Bebko-Jones, Linda (D-Erie)	Senate admin. asst., case worker
Bishop, Louise Williams (D-Philadelphia)	Baptist Evangelist minister
Cohen, Lita Indzel (R-Montgomery)	attorney, businesswoman
Dailey, Mary Ann D'Altorio (R-Montgomery)	college prof.; registered nurse
Forcier, Teresa E. Brown (R-Crawford)	asst. dir. cnty. tax claim bureau
Harhart, Julie (R-Lehigh, Northampton)	legislative aide

207

Josephs, Babette (D-Philadelphia)	attorney
Laughlin, Susan (D-Allegheny, Beaver)	community volunteer
Lederer, Marie A. (D-Philadelphia)	college teacher, gov't manager
Major, Sandra J. (R-Sullivan, Susquehanna, Wyoming)	former county treasurer
Manderino, Kathy M. (D-Philadelphia)	attorney
Mann, Jennifer L. (D-Lehigh)	former business owner
Miller, Sheila M. (R-Berks)	newspaper editor, conservationist
Mundy, Phyllis Block (D-Luzerne)	business manager
Orie, Jane Clare (R-Allegheny)	attorney
Rubley, Carole A. Drumm (R-Chester)	environmental consultant
Seyfert, Ph.D. R. Tracy (R-Erie, Crawford)	psychologist
Steelman, Ph.D. Sara Gerling (D-Indiana)	college psych researcher/teacher
Taylor, Elinor Gene Zimmerman (R-Chester)	college professor
True, Katie Buck (R-Lancaster)	substance abuse writer, TELLS tutor
Vance, Patricia Huston (R-Cumberland)	registered nurse
Washington, LeAnna M. (D-Philadelphia)	human services
Williams, Constance "Connie" Hess (D-Montgomery)	congressional aide
Youngblood, Rosita C. (D-Philadelphia)	constituent serv. rep., credit adm.

2001-2002

Baker, Jane S. (R-Lehigh)	county commissioner, executive
Bard, Ellen M. (R-Montgomery)	business owner, twnshp. com.

Bebko-Jones, Linda (D-Erie)	Senate admin. asst., case worker
Bishop, Louise Williams (D-Philadelphia)	Baptist Evangelist minister
Cohen, Lita Indzel (R-Montgomery)	attorney, businesswoman
Dailey, Mary Ann D'Altorio (R-Montgomery)	college prof.; registered nurse
Forcier, Teresa E. Brown (R-Crawford)	asst. dir. cnty. tax claim bureau
Harhart, Julie (R-Lchigh, Northampton)	legislative aide
Harper, Catherine M. "Kate" (R-Mongomery)	attorney
Josephs, Babette (D-Philadelphia)	attorney
Laughlin, Susan (D-Allegheny, Beaver)	community volunteer
Lederer, Marie A. (D-Philadelphia)	college teacher, gov't manager
Macereth, Beverly L. (R-York)	mayor, agency exec. director
Major, Sandra J. (R-Sullivan, Susquehanna, Wyoming)	former county treasurer
Manderino, Kathy M. (D-Philadelphia)	attorney
Mann, Jennifer L. (D-Lehigh)	former business owner
Miller, Sheila M. (R-Berks)	newspaper editor, conservationist
Mundy, Phyllis Block (D-Luzerne)	business manager
Orie, Jane Clare (R-Allegheny)	attorney
Pickett, Tina L. (R-Bradford)	restaurant and hotel owner
Rubley, Carole A. Drumm (R-Chester)	environmental consultant
Steelman, Ph.D. Sara Gerling (D-Indiana)	college psych researcher/teacher

209

Taylor, Elinor Gene Zimmerman
(R-Chester) college professor
Vance, Patricia Huston (R-Cumberland) registered nurse
Washington, LeAnna M. (D-Philadelphia) human services
Watson, Katherine M. (R-Bucks) county admin., teacher

Williams, Constance "Connie" Hess
(D-Montgomery) congressional aide
Youngblood, Rosita C. (D-Philadelphia) constituent serv. rep.,
credit adm.

Appendix III
Women in the House by County

COUNTY	MEMBER	YEARS REPRESENTED
Allegheny	Grimes, Helen	1923-1930
	Gillette, Helen D.	1967-1978
	Kernick, Phyllis T.	1975-1980
	Heiser, Loraine "Lori"	1981-1982
	Langtry, Alice S.	1985-1992
	Farmer, Elaine F.	1987-1996
	Laughlin, Susan	1993-
	Burns, Barbara A.	1994-
	Orie, Jane Clare	1997-
Beaver	Laughlin, Susan	1989-
Berks	Wilson, Lilith M.	1931-1936
	Miller, Sheila M.	1993-
Bradford	Sirianni, Carmel A.	1983-1988
	Pickett, Tina L.	2001-
Bucks	Kooker, Margarette S.	1955-1966
	Fawcett, Charlotte D.	1973-1976
	George, Margaret H. "Peg"	1977-1980
	Wilson, Jean T.	1989-1992
	Watson, Katherine M.	2001-
Butler	MacKinney, Sarah Gertrude	1923-1924
	Carone, Patricia Ann [Krebs]	1991-1998
Cambria	Gallagher, Ph.D. Sarah McCune	1923-1924
	Clark, Rita	1979-1980
	Telek, Leona G.	1989-1992

211

	Steelman, Ph.D. Sara Gerling	1993-
Centre	Wise, D.Ed. Helen Dickerson	1977-1978
	Rudy, Ruth Corman	1983-1996
Chester	Thomas, Martha G.	1923-1926
	Crawford, Patricia A.	1969-1976
	Taylor, Elinor Gene Zimmerman	1977-
	Rubley, Carole A. Drumm	1993-
Clinton	Donahue, Ruth Stover	1955-1960
Crawford	Bentley, Alice M.	1923-1928
	Maine, Constance G. "Connie"	1987-1990
	Forcier, Teresa E. Brown	1991-
	Seyfert, Ph.D. Tracy R.	1997-2000
Cumberland	George, Lourene Walker	1963-1970
	Vance, Patricia Huston	1991-
Delaware	Kernaghan, Mae Winter	1957-1970
	Odorisio, Helen R.	1967-1968
	Whittlesey, Faith Ryan	1973-1975
	Arty, Mary Ann [Majors]	1979-1988
	Durham, Kathrynann Walrath	1979-1996
Erie	Bebko-Jones, Linda	1993-
	Seyfert, Ph. D. Tracy R.	1997-2000
Fayette	Adams, Ella Collier	1927-1930
Indiana	Steelman, Ph.D. Sara Gerling	1991-
Lackawanna	Munley, Marion L.	1947-1964
Lancaster	Horting, Ruth Grigg	1937-1938
	Honaman, June N.	1977-1988
	True, Katie Buck	1993-2000

Lawrence	Carone, Patricia A. [Krebs]	1991-1998
Lehigh	Markley, Marian E.	1951-1968
	Leiby, Mary E.	1955-1956
	Ritter, Karen A.	1987-1994
	McHale, Katherine Pecka	1991-1992
	Boscola, Lisa M.	1995-1998
	Harhart, Julie	1995-
	Mann, Jennifer L.	1999-
	Baker, Jane S.	2001-
Luzerne	Mundy, Phyllis Block	1991-
Mercer	Dye, Jeanette M.	1945-1950
Mifflin	Rudy, Ruth Corman	1983-1996
Montgomery	Kirkbride, Mabelle M.	1929-1932
	Crawford, Evelyn Glazier Henzel	1955-1962
	Brugger, Jeanne D.	1965-1966
	Fawcett, Charlotte D.	1971-1976
	Lewis, Marilyn Stoughton	1979-1982
	Hagarty, Lois Sherman	1980-1992
	Harley, Ellen A.	1991-1994
	Cohen, Lita Indzel	1993-
	Bard, Ellen M.	1995-
	Sheehan, Ph.D. Colleen A.	1995-1996
	Williams, Constance Hess "Connie"	1997-
	Dailey, Mary Ann D'Altorio	1999-
	Harper, Catherine M. "Kate"	2001-
Northampton	Reibman, Jeanette F.	1955-1956, 1959-1966
	McHale, Katherine Pecka	1991-1992
	Boscola, Lisa M.	1995-1998
	Harhart, Julie	1995-

Philadelphia	deYoung, Rosa Stein	1923-1924
	Speiser, Martha G.	1923-1924
	Pitts, Lillie H.	1923-1932
	Pennock, Martha M.	1925-1934
	Brancato, Anna M.[Wood]	1933-1940, 1945-1946
	Fauset, Crystal Bird	1939-1940
	Coyle, Josephine C.	1945-1946, 1951-1954
	Varallo, Mary A.	1945-1946, 1949-1960
	McCosker, Henrietta C.	1947-1948
	Monroe, Susie	1949-1968
	Pashley, Kathryn Graham	1955-1966
	Anderson, Sarah A.	1955-1972
	Duffy, Mary Alice	1957-1958
	Miller, Beatrice Z.	1957-1960
	Jones, Frances R.	1959-1966
	Winter, Elizabeth A. Watson	1963-1964
	Kelly, Anita Palermo	1963-1978
	Toll, Rose Ornstein	1971-1976
	Scanlon, Agnes Ruddock	1977-1978
	Harper, Ruth B.	1977-1992
	Weston, Frances Peteraf	1981-1990
	Josephs, Babette	1985-
	Kitchen, Shirley M.	1987-1988
	Bishop, Louise Williams	1989-
	McHugh, Connie Black	1991-1992
	Washington, LeAnna M.	1993-
	Manderino, Kathy M.	1993-
	Lederer, Marie A.	1993-
	Youngblood, Rosita C.	1994-
Somerset	Telek, Leona G.	1989-1992
Sullivan	Sirianni, Carmel A.	1975-1988
	Major, Sandra J.	1995-

214

Susquehanna	Sirianni, Carmel A.	1975-1988
	Major, Sandra J.	1995-
Westmoreland	Trescher, Maud Byers	1925-1926
	Denman, Mary Thompson	1931-1932
Wyoming	Wynd, Elizabeth Steele	1961-1966
	Sirianni, Carmel A.	1975-1988
	Major, Sandra J.	1995-
York	Alexander, Jane M.	1965-1968
	Mackereth, Beverly L.	2001-

Appendix IV
Women in the House
Whose Husbands Also Served in the House
(Includes Special Elections of Widows)

Donahue, Ruth Stover (R-Clinton)1955-60. Her husband, **Charles E. Donahue**, served in the House 1939-40, and in the state Senate 1919-22.

George, Lourene Walker (R-Cumberland) 1963-70. Her husband, **Arthur George**, served in the House from 1949-50 and again from 1955-62.

Jones, Frances R. (D-Philadelphia) 1959-66 was elected in special election May 19, 1959 to replace her husband, **Granville E. Jones**, who served from 1949-59 and who died March 7, 1959.

Kelly, Anita Palermo (D-Philadelphia) 1963-78 was elected on November 5, 1963 to fill the unexpired term of her husband, **William J. Kelly**, who served from 1961-63, and who died in 1963. She was reelected in 1964 and served successive terms until 1978.

Laughlin, Susan (D-Allegheny) 1989-__ replaced her husband, **Charles P. Laughlin**, who served from 1973-88 and died April 10, 1988. She was elected in the fall general election as a write-in candidate.

McHale, Katherine Pecka (D-Lehigh) 1991-92, replaced her husband **Paul McHale** who served from 1983-91, in a special election on May 21, 1991 following his election to the United States Congress.

Munley, Marion L. (D-Lackawanna) 1947-64, replaced her husband **Robert W. Munley**, who served from 1939-47 and died in 1947, in a special election on September 9, 1947.

Odorisio, Helen R. (R-Delaware) 1967-68, replaced her husband, **Rocco A. Odorisio**, who served from 1959-67 and died April 5, 1967. She was elected in a special election on July 25, 1967.

Speiser, Martha G. (R-Philadelphia) 1923-24, followed her husband, **Maurice J. Speiser**, who served in the House from 1913-14. They served non-consecutive terms.

Telek, Leona G. (R-Cambria, Somerset) 1989-92, followed her husband, **William Telek**, who was murdered in Harrisburg in May of 1988, through her election in the fall 1988 general election.

Wilson, Jean T. (R-Bucks) 1989-92, followed her husband, **Benjamin H. Wilson**, who served in the House from 1966-88, and who died on March 6, 1988, through her election in the general election in the fall of 1988.

Wynd, Elizabeth S. (R-Wyoming) 1961-66, followed her husband, **James Wynd, Jr.**, who served from 1957-61, who died on March 28,1961. She was elected in a special election on May 16, 1961.

Other Special Elections of Women

Burns, Barbara A. (D-Allegheny) who served in 1994 only, was elected in a special election held on March 7, 1994, to replace **Thomas J. Murphy Jr.,** who served from 1979-94 and who resigned to become mayor of Pittsburgh.

Hagarty, Lois Sherman (R-Montgomery) 1980-92, was

elected in a special election held on March 11, 1980, to replace **Anthony J. Scirica**, who served from 1971-80, and who resigned to accept a judical post.

Kitchen, Shirley M. (D-Philadelphia) 1987-88, was elected in a special election to replace **Alphonso Deal**, who served from 1981-87, and who died on June 3, 1987.

Washington, LeAnna M. (D-Philadlephia) 1993-__, replaced **Gordon Linton**, who resigned to accept an appointment in Washington, D.C. She was elected in a special election held on November 2, 1993.

Youngblood, Rosita C. (D-Philadelphia) 1994-__, replaced **Robert O'Donnell**, who resigned to return to his legal practice. She was elected in a special election on April 5, 1994.

Works Cited

Works Cited

100 Years of Leadership: Pennsylvania House of Representatives' Caucus Officers 1900 until Today, Pennsylvania House of Representatives, Speaker's Office. Harrisburg: December 1998:25.

A Great Idea: The League of Women Voters 1920-Present. Washington, D.C.: n.p.,1984. A&E Biography Online. 1999. Cambridge University Press. 28 Oct 1999. http:// www.biography.com.

Adler, Emily Stier and J. Stanley Lemons. The Elect: Rhode Island's Women Legislators, 1922-1990, Providence: League of Rhode Island Historical Societies: 11.

Administrative Code of 1929, "The Osteoporosis Amendment," 1998, P.L. 511, No. 71.

Allentown Morning Call, "Mrs. Marian Markley, ex-state legislator," obit. 28 Jan 1986.

And Still They Persevered... A Brief History. University of Maryland. 1994. National Women's History Project. 12 Oct 1999. http://www.infrm.umd.edu.

Associated Press, The Patriot-News, "Women find low rate of progress," 9 Jan 01:B.

Baer, John M. Philadelphia Daily News, "Don't look for a gift horse in Harrisburg," 25 Jun 1990:13.

Baer, John. Philadelphia Daily News, "They'd triple own pensions with little to fear, Phila. Lawmakers lead the charge," 4 Dec 1990:20.

Baldwin, Bonnie. Delaware County Daily Times, "Mrs. Arty has difficulty quitting," 29 Jan 1979:7.

Beaver County Times, "Women noticeably absent in government: 8 Jan 2001: n.p.

Beers, Paul. First Black Woman Legislator, Rep. Crystal Bird Fauset, unpublished manuscript, 17 Jan 1988.

Beers, Paul. Pennsylvania Politics Today and Yesterday, Pennsylvania State University Press: University Park and London, 1980:101.

Biebel, Mary Theresa. Wilkes-Barre Times Leader, "The 75th anniversary of the Women Suffrage Movement Amendment is Saturday. Some women say there's more to be gained." 22 Aug 1995.

Black Legislators in Pennsylvania's History (1911-1993), Pennsylvania Legislative Black Caucus:n.d.:17.

Brosius, Shirley G. Sunday Patriot-News, "Rep. Vance calls on women to get involved in community," 15 Nov 1998:B6.

221

Burnham, Carrie S. Woman Suffrage. The Argument of Carrie S. Burnham before Chief Justice Reed, and Associate Justices Agnew, Sharwwood and Mercur of the Supreme Court of Pennsylvania, en Banc. 3rd and 4th of Apr 1873. Philadelphia, Citizen's Suffrage Association, 1873:7.

Butler Eagle, "'T.W. Phipps Wins Race for Congress, Miss MacKinney and Woner Cop Assembly Contest," 8 Nov 1922:1.

Butler Eagle, Butler, "T. W. Phillips Wins Race for Congress, Miss MacKinney and Woner Cop Assembly Contest. 8 Nov 1922:1.

Byrnes, James F. 3rd Delaware County Daily Times, "We have 'Faith' in the House," 8 Nov 1972:14.

Calpin, John C. The Evening Bulletin, "Rep. Varallo honored for aid to Italian migration to U.S." 6 Feb 1958: n.p.

Cambria County Historical Society, "Sarah McCune Gallagher: Internationally-known Educator and Conscious Political Leader," N.d.;n.d.

Capitolwire. "Orie to be featured in national 'Women in Politics' documentary," internet version, 6 Apr 2000.

Capitolwire. "Rep. Orie legislation designed to ease impact of Allegheny County reassessment," 31 Aug 2000.

Center for the American Woman and Politics (CAWP), Eagleton Institute of Politics, Rutgers University, NJ, telephone interview, Nov 2000.

Centre Daily Times, "Rudy campaign ends with lopsided victory," 7 Nov 1990:B1.

Centre Daily Times, "Rudy endorsed by gun association," 3 Nov 1998:n.p.

Chaffin, Susan. VOICES, The Kansas Collection Online Magazine, "We Will Vote!, Fall 1977.

Charles, Tom. Governor's Press Office Press Release, "Gov. Ridge Nominates Kathrynann Durham to Delaware County Judicial Vacancy," 10 Oct 2000.

Chastain, Sue. Philadelphia Inquirer, "She charms them right out of their votes," 4 Jun 1978:n.p.

Coatesville Record, "Three incumbents are challenged in County legislative races," 4 Nov 1972:1.

Cohen, Lita Indzel. Legislation-Prime Sponsorship 1999-2000 Legislative Session, unpublished list, n.d.:1-3.

Cohen, Lita, unpublished biography, 23 Jan 2001

Collins, Herman Leroy and Wilfred Jordan, Philadelphia: A Story of Progress. 4 vols. Philadelphia: Lewis Hist. Pub. Co., 1941. FLP#R974.81C.69. (Room Ref.):327.

Commerce and Trade (12 PA. C.S.)- Amend European Union Member. 1988, P.L. 939, No.122.

Cooney, Tom. Philadelphia Daily News, "Phila. Sticks by House Dems," 5 Nov 1980:11.

Daily Times, "Mae Kernaghan, first women legislator in Pa., dies at 79," 30 Sep 1980.

Delaware County Daily Times, "Durham blitzes Tilghman on vets issues," 9 Nov 1988:41.

Delaware County Daily Times, "Mrs. Odorisio Wins in Special Election, 26 Jul 1967:1.

Delaware County Daily Times, "Ralph Garzia loses, blames GOP literature," 8 Nov 1978:12.

Delaware County Sunday Times, "Jeanne D. Brugger, 75, former state legislators," obit. 12 Apr 1992:40.

Diskin, Meg. Delaware County Daily Times, "Durham survives in 160th district: Incumbent claims eighth term despite Buffington attacks," 4 Nov 1992:40.

Distinguished Daughters of Pennsylvania, 46th Annual Presentation Luncheon Program, 26 Oct 1994.

Distinguished Daughters of Pennsylvania, luncheon program, n.p., 1999.

Easton Express, "Bucchin Is Victor In Bethlehem as GOP Is Blanked," 3 Nov 1954:1.

Easton Express, "Democrats Win Greatest Hold on Congress," 5 Nov 1958:1.

Easton Express, "Three Lawmakers In Area Named Unit Chairmen, Mrs. Reibman Heads Education Committee of Lower House," 7 Jan 1959:1.

Ebbeat, Stephanie. The Patriot-News, "Sen. Peterson denies charges of harassment; blames foe for controversy," 16 Oct 1996:B1.

Ellis, Harold D. Delaware County Daily Times, "House ok's delay in pay hikes," 7 Feb 1979:1.

Ellis, Harold D. Delaware County Daily Times, "Legislators have many proposals," 15 Jan 1973:1.

Esbri, Lioda. Women's Commission Directory, Forward. Harrisburg: n.p., 1999.

Eshelman, Russell E. Jr. Philadelphia Inquirer, "All work and free play for two legislators," 10 Dec 1992:B3.

Eshelman, Russell E. Jr. Philadelphia Inquirer, "New PA Statehouse Ranks 45th in Gender..." 27 Jan 1997:B1.

Fazollah, Mark. Philadelphia Inquirer, "Deal's Seat Goes to Democrat," 4 Nov 1987:A12.

Feeney, Thomas C. Delaware County Daily Times, "Arty steps down, Williams takes reigns," 4 Jan 1995:6.

Feldman, Linda. The Christian Science Monitor, "Election coverage of women: more personality, less on issues," 25 Oct 1999.

Fifty Years Old and Proud of It. Philadelphia: n.p., 1970:11.

First Convention Minutes, First Annual Convention of the Pennsylvania State Council of Republican Women, 12-14 Nov 1923:6.

First Convention Program, First Annual Convention of the Pennsylvania State Council of Republican Women, 12-14 Nov 1923.

Foley, Eileen. The Evening Bulletin, "The Go-Go-Go life of Mary Varallo," 12 Apr 1958:n.p.

Foster, Ph.D. Joseph S. interview, 26 Feb 1999.

Gatek, Andi. Delaware County Daily Times, "Will Arty take Curt's seat?" 6 Nov 1986:5.

Gattone, Jane. Delaware County Daily Times," ... then there's Mr. Whittlesey," 8 Nov 1972:1.

Gibb, Tom. The Patriot-News, "Peterson thumps Rudy in the 5th," 6 Nov 1996:B10.

Godcharles, Frederic A. Litt.D. Encyclopedia of Pennsylvania Biography, "Pennock, Martha M." EPB XXII 109. New York: Lewis Historical Publishing Company, Inc. 1957.

Grace, Joseph. Philadelphia Daily News, "Putting up slates to redraw on," 7 Mar 1990.

Grey Towers National Historic Landmark. Home page. 12 Oct 1999. Keyword: Cornelia Pinchot.

Gurnett, Kate. Albany Times Union, "Women's Rights: It all began in 1848." 12 Jul 1998.

Hain, Peg. Interview, Nov 1999.

Harrisburg Telegraph, 2 Jan 1923:8.

Highlights of a Half Century: The League of Women Voters of Pennsylvania 1920-1970. Philadelphia: n.p.,1970.

Hine, Darlene Clark. Black Women in America. An Historical Encyclopedia, vol. I. Brooklyn, New York: Carlson Publishing Inc., 1993:410,411.

Hollister, H.J. The Pittsburgh Post, "Pinchot Fires Parting Shot Before Assembly," 5 Jan 1927:1.

Horle, Ph.D., Craig W. interview, 26 Feb 1999.

House Journal, 24 Nov 1998.

House of Representatives Legislative Directory, 1925-30; 1935-38; 1949-50; 1953-1968; 1975-2000. House of Representatives.

House Resolutions, unpublished list:5.

Howard, Liliane S. "Philadelphia County Woman Suffrage Society," unpublished manuscript, 1945:2.

Huber, Dave. Mountaineer-Herald, "A Woman of Distinction," 25 Feb 1987:n.p.

Intellegencer Journal, "June Honaman 74, GOP leader, 6-term state rep of 97th District," obit. 5 Dec 1994:B3.

Intelligencer Journal, "Ruth Horting, 88, was state welfare secretary," obit. 10 Oct 1988.

Irwin, Inez Haines. Angels and Amazons. Garden City, New York: Doubleday, Doran and Company, Inc.:249.

Jensen, Edward. Pittsburgh Post Gazette, "Legislature Opens Amid Feuding, Confusion," 2 Jan 1979:1.

John, Robert. The Tribune Democrat, "Clark, Telek, Yahner, Stewart House Victors," 8 Nov 1978:27.

Johnson, Mark E. Lancaster Intelligencer Journal, "It's still hard for Women to get invited to electoral party" 1 Nov 1999: n.p.

Johnson, Tyree. Philadelphia Daily News, "Kitchen already gets heat," 4 Nov 1987:41.

Jones, Bill. The Tribune Democrat, "Earned victory, Lee Telek says," 10 Nov 1988:B1.

Keegan, Frank. Easton Express Times, "Double standard raises questions, Boscola raises hell," 12 Mar 2000.

Keller, Frances K. History of Lancaster County, "Ruth Grigg Horting," N.d., n.p.

Keyser, Lynn. Delaware County Daily Times, "Springfield Republican defeats Stapleton," 8 Nov 1978:12.

Klaus, Mary. The Patriot-News, "State women trail peers, report says," 9 Nov 1998:1.

Krebs, Jeanette. The Patriot-News, "Women's Commission to Disband," 5 May 1996.

LaTorre, David. Allentown Morning Call, "Pennsylvania low in percentage of women lawmakers," 8 Jun 01:n.p.

Legislative Journal of the Pennsylvania House of Representatives, 2 Jan 1923:n.p.

Legislative Journal of the Pennsylvania House of Representatives, 28 Feb 1923:350.

Letter to Speaker of the House Matthew J. Ryan, 19 Apr 1999.

Lewis, Betty. Coatesville Record, "Rep. Crawford defeats John Shea," 6 Nov 1974:2.

Lewis, Claude. Philadelphia Inquirer, "Whitman can't ignore blacks now. Rollins' kickback-and-tell story puts the pressure on the governor-elect," 15 Nov 1993:A15.

Lighting the Way. Harrisburg: n.p., 1999:3.

Liquor Code-Omnibus Amendments, 1996, P.L. 312, No. 49.

Loeb, Vernon. Philadelphia Inquirer, "After state cuts funding, will abortion rate change?" 31 Jul 1981:B1.

Lyon, Ellen. The Patriot-News, "Rudy on 8th convention trip," 8 Aug 2000.

Marion Munley, unpublished manuscript, n.d.

Mayor, Mara. Connecticut Review, "Fears and Fantasies of the anti-Suffragists." 7th ed. No. 2, Apr 1974:64, 65.

McElroy, Ph.D. Janice H. Pennsylvania Women in History, Our Hidden Heritage. American Association of University Women. 2nd ed. Jun 1983:XV.

McKinney, Mattie. Black Legislators in Pennsylvania 1911-2000, Pennsylvania Legislative Black Caucus, n.d.:49.

McQuillen, Laurence. USA TODAY, "Study: Bias against female candidates." 10 Oct 1999.

Mease, Carl L. and Carol Yulich. Women in the Pennsylvania Legislature (1922-1997), "Preface," Pennsylvania Legislative Reference Bureau.

More Women Candidates. Camp Hill: n.p., 1988.

Morrison, Helen. Delaware County Daily Times, "Arty Dumps Davis, Retains 165th seat," 3 Nov 1982:10.

Moving up to the National Stage: Organizing Women's Votes. Internet:1.

Neri, Albert J. Erie Times-News, "Women are making political strides, but very slowly," 22 Jun 1997.

New Age, "Elizabeth W. Wallace," 31 Jan 1974:2.

Newill, Bill. Bucks County Courier Times, "George leaves Ferguson's head spinning – again," 8 Nov 1978:A12.

Nicholson, Jim. Philadelphia Daily News, "Sarah Anderson, 91; Ex-Pa Representative," obit. 11 Dec 1992.

Ovenshine, Gordon, Tribune-Review, "State has few female politicians," 3 Apr 2000: n.p.

Oxford Times, "Miss Thomas Received First Prize," 15 Jan 1925.

Pelikan, Betty A. Women of Cambria County: Their Work-Their History-Their Contributions 1770-1987, "The Gallagher Sisters," Johnstown Branch, American Association of University Women, A.G. Halldin Publishing Company: Indiana, Pa.:196.

Pennsylvania Elected Women's Association Bylaws, Article II. Adopted 4 Apr 1981. Pennsylvania State Archives.

Pennsylvania House of Representatives "Class of 2001-2002," House Republican Communications Department, Jan 2001.

Pennsylvania Manuals. vols. 97-113. Department of General Services.

Pennsylvania State Council of Republican Women By-Laws, Adopted 28 Feb 1923.

Pennsylvania State Council of Republican Women. Meeting minutes, 27 Feb 1923.

Pennsylvania Women's Campaign Fund News, Hazleton: n.p., 1993.

Pennsylvania Women's Campaign Fund. State College: Barash Advertising, 1982.

Pennsylvania Women's Political Network, "Moving More Women into Public Office:" Internet website.

Philadelphia Inquirer, "Connie B. McHugh, 58, activist," obit 21 Sep 1997:D14.

Philadelphia Inquirer, "Crystal Fauset Dies, Set Mark in Legislature," 30 Mar 1965.

Philadelphia Inquirer, "K. Pashley, 70, Served in State House," 4 Dec 1981:C18.

Philadelphia Inquirer, "Mrs. Beatrice Miller, 83, Former Legislator," obit. 27 Sep 1975.

Philadelphia Inquirer, "Mrs. M. Speiser, 89, modern art collector," obit. 24 Sep 1968:n.p.

Philadelphia Inquirer, "Mrs. McCosker Dies, Served in Legislature," n.d.

Philadelphia Inquirer, "Pennsylvania House Votes by Wards," 8 Nov 1944:4.

Philadelphia Inquirer, "Susie Monroe, Legislator, Dies at Age 89," n.d.

Pinchot, Gifford. The Ladies Home Journal, "The Influence of Women in Politics," Sep 1922:12.

Pittsburgh Post-Gazette, "Mary Denman, 76, ex-Pa. Ex-Legislator," obit. 22 Oct 1975:n.p.

Pittsburgh Post-Gazette, "Post Gazette Endorsements," 6 Nov 1978:6.

Pittsburgh Press, "Mt. Lebanon Attorney Mary Denman Dies," 12 Oct 1975:n.p.

Pottstown Mercury, "Marilyn Lewis wins second term in House," 5 Nov 1980:26.

Pottstown Mercury, "Newly elected legislator, Evelyn Henzel outlines civic duties to Century Club," n.d.:18.

Pratt, William C. The Pennsylvania Magazine, "Women and American Socialism: The Reading Experience," vol. 99, 1975:72-91.

Project 70 Lands-Sale of Montg. Co. Lands Free of Restrictions, 1994, P.L. 68, No. 4.

Reabuck, Sandra K. The Tribune Democrat, "Telek not resting on her laurels," 8 Nov 1990.

Rego, Paul. History of Women's Organizations in Pennsylvania, unpublished manuscript, Millersville University, 8 Dec 1999.

Ritter, Karen. "Women's History Information," unpublished manuscript, 23 Jan 2001.

Rowe, Karen. The York Dispatch, "Remember the ladies, Gov. Ridge," 11 Mar 1997.

Roy, Daniel J. The Intelligencer, "Wilson wins second House term," 7 Nov 1991:A3.

Ryan, Speaker Matthew J., interview, 8 Aug 2000.

228

Sabatini, Richard V. Philadelphia Inquirer, "Mary F. Varallo, former legislator," obit. 28 Nov 1979:n.p.

Sanders, John A. 100 Years After Emancipation: History of the Philadelphia Negro, 1787-1963, n.p. F.R.S. Publishing Co., 1968. FLP#326Sa8750 Free Library of Philadelphia.

Sataline, Suzanne. Philadelphia Inquirer, "Party picks Street Aide," 12 Sep 1996:B1.

Seelye, Katherine. Philadelphia Inquirer, "Ruling bumps Duffy from ballot for court," 6 Apr 1993:B3.

Seventy-five Suffragists, University of Maryland, National Women's History Project, 12 Oct 1999. <http://www.inform.umd.edu/EdRes/Topic/WomensStudies/Reading Room/.../75-suggragists.htm>.

Shaffer, Michelle. The Meadville Tribune, "Maine wins sixth district seat," 5 Nov 1986:1.

Sheehan, Kathy. Philadelphia Daily News, "N.Phila. resident vow not to be dumped on," 10 Mar 1988:29.

Shuster, William G. Bucks County Courier Times, "Fawcett defeats Walters," 6 Nov 1972:14.

Shuster, William G. Bucks County Courier Times, "THE UPSET: Peg George beats odds... and Ferguson," 3 Nov 1976:B17.

Silver, Jonathan D. and Milan Simonich. Pittsburgh Port-Gazette, "Dole facing 2 centuries of male prejudices," 6 Jan 1999.

Smith, Elmer. Philadelphia Daily News, "Locale Issue Was a Big Factor," 24 Apr 1966:6.

Smith, Jane. The Meadville Tribune, "Connie Maine Outdistances Jim DiMaria," 9 Nov 1988:1.

Smull's Biographical Sketches of Members 1923-24.

Smull's Legislative Handbook, 1927, Biographical Sketches of Representatives, n.p.:1993.

Speaker's Office, Pennsylvania House of Representatives. Harrisburg:1998:18.

Spiers, Nan. The Patriot-News, "Commission for Women reinvigorated," letter to the Editor, 16 Apr 1997.

Spiers, Nan. The Patriot-News, letter to the editor, 4 Apr 1997.

Standing Committees of the House of Representatives 2001-2002 Session, Office of the Chief Clerk, 24 Jan 2001.

229

State Legislatures Magazine, "Women in the Legislature: Numbers Inch up Nationwide," "Jan 1999:9.

Stauffer, Cindy. Lancaster New Era, "Breathalyzer to go. Law requires ignition lock for drunk drivers," 2 Sep 2000.

Stone, Sherry. Philadelphia Tribune, "From lace to legislation, Harper's hallmark is style," n.d. 1992.

Strauss, Robert. Philadelphia Daily News, "State Senate," 17 May 1978.

Sunday Patriot-News, "A look at the status of women," 28 Feb 1999:2.

The Evening Bulletin, "Mrs. Rosa de Young Dies; Early Woman Legislator," 23 Jun 1955.

The Evening News, "Eight Female Members Are Pleased to Have Men Smoke; No Feminine Bloc Planned," 4 Jan 1923.

The Gazette and Daily, "Senate race in doubt: Gailey, Alexander Win," 9 Nov 1966:1.

The Gazette and Daily, "Three County Democrats Win in Races for Assembly Seats," 4 Nov 1964: 1.

The History Channel Online. 1999. History Channel Exhibits: Women's Suffrage. 12 Oct 1999. http://www.historychannel.com/.

The Intelligencer Record, "Margarette Kooker, 1st Bucks woman in House," 25 Mar 1990:c.

The Morning Herald, "Fisher wins in Fayette County by Three to One," 4 Nov 1926:1.

The Morning Herald,, "Election results," 8 Nov 1928:13.

The New Hope Gazette, "Voters Guide," 15 May 1958:4.

The Patriot, "Women Legislators to be Greeted Today." 2 Jan 1923.

The Patriot, Harrisburg, 9 Nov 1922:1.

The Patriot-News, "Inside the Capitol," 21 Aug 2000:A4.

The Pennsylvania Federation of Democratic Women. Harrisburg: 1999:n.p.

The Reading Eagle, "Woman legislator holds first public post after 23 years in political life," 6 Jan 1931.

The Scranton Times, "Former State Legislator Dies; Mother of Lawyer and Judge," 15 Sep 1983:10.

The Status of Women in Pennsylvania: Highlights, Institute for Women's Policy Research, George Washington University, Feb 1999.

The Sullivan Review, "Carmel Sirianni," 25 Apr 1991:4.

The Sullivan Review, "Off-Year voters give Harrison victory over Nelligan in 11th Congressional District," 4 Nov 1982:1.

The Tribune Democrat, "Democrats' Grip Eased in Cambria," 9 Nov 1978:31.

The Weekly Bulletin, "Jane Alexander wins seat in State Legislature," 11 Nov 1964:1.

Tigue, Colleen. A Study of the Demographics of the 101 Women in the Pennsylvania House of Representatives, East Stroudsburg University of Pennsylvania, 24 Apr 2000.

Trescher, Maude B. The News-Dispatch, "Women Legislators Welcome Everywhere Except in Secret Conferences," 8 Jan 1925:1.

Twyman, Anthony S. Philadelphia Daily News, "It's a grave matter to McHugh," 31 Oct 1992:17.

Van Every, Dale. Butler Eagle, "Women In Penna. State Legislature to Work with Men, Idea of 'Feminine Bloc' is Scouted by All in Summary of Their Views," 1 Jan 1923:1.

Wallace, Andy. Philadelphia Inquirer, "Rose Toll; served 6 years in Pa. House," 14 May 1997:B6.

Wallace, Andy. Philadelphia Inquirer, "Sara Duffy, 64; Founded First Women's Law Firm," 6 Oct 1992:A8.

Who's Who in Pennsylvania, vol. 1. Chicago: A.N. Marcus Company, 1939:1897.

Wiegand, Harold J. Philadelphia Inquirer, "Whittlesey follows a tradition," 28 Sep 1981:A15.

Women Legislators of Maryland, Internet. Maryland State Archives, 27 Jan 1998.

Women Members of the House of Representatives Survey, Speaker's Office, 2 Apr 1999.

Women Members of the Pennsylvania House of Representatives Survey, Office of Speaker of the House Matthew J. Ryan, Harrisburg, 2 Apr 1999.

Yulich, Carol. Women in the Pennsylvania Legislature 1922-1997. Harrisburg: Legislative Reference Bureau, March 1998:13.